LATER LETTERS
OF
LADY AUGUSTA STANLEY

LADY AUGUSTA STANLEY
From a Drawing by Richmond

LATER LETTERS
OF
LADY AUGUSTA STANLEY
1864-1876

Including many unpublished Letters to
and from Queen Victoria and correspondence with Dean Stanley, her
sister, Lady Frances Baillie, and others

Edited by

THE DEAN OF WINDSOR
and
HECTOR BOLITHO

JONATHAN CAPE
THIRTY BEDFORD SQUARE
LONDON

FIRST PUBLISHED MCMXXIX

PRINTED IN GREAT BRITAIN BY
BUTLER & TANNER LTD
FROME

ILLUSTRATIONS

Editors' Note.

The first volume of Lady Augusta Stanley's Letters, published in 1927, covered the period of her life spent as Lady-in-Waiting to the Duchess of Kent and Bedchamber Woman to Queen Victoria.

This second volume describes her life from her marriage to Dean Stanley in 1864 to her death in 1876.

THE EDITORS wish to acknowledge their indebtedness to *The Life of Dean Stanley* by Rowland E. Prothero, M.A. (now Lord Ernle), *The Letters and Journals of Queen Victoria* (John Murray), *The Life of Julius and Mary Mohl,* and to letters supplied by Lord Stanley of Alderley and Mrs. Henry Cust, for certain references and quotations in the text and in footnotes in this volume.

CONTENTS

7

CONTENTS

8

CONTENTS

CONTENTS

INTRODUCTION

When my friend Mr. Bolitho and I edited the first volume of Lady Augusta Stanley's Letters, we did so simply because that series of letters to her sister possessed a peculiar charm and interest which seemed to belong to the world, not only as illustrating a period of history, but because they revealed a singularly beautiful character. But we made no attempt to write a biography, or to bring in any other lights on Lady Augusta's life.

Our picture was confined to the relationship between Lady Augusta and her sister. The glimpses of Court life were incidental and our selection of the letters was governed by that fact. We did not propose to write the story of the Duchess of Kent, or of Queen Victoria, but to show the character of Lady Augusta, although the fact that she was at Court during all the time when she was writing these letters, naturally brought the Royal Family as characters into her story.

But that first series of letters gave so many people a vivid interest in her personality, that we were bombarded with requests to give the picture of her married life. Those requests came from far afield, and even old courtiers in Coburg remembered the qualities of her character and the wisdom and humour of her conversation and expressed their interest in the story of her life as wife of the Dean.

At first we refused. Although they continued regularly, the letters to my mother in the second period were not of a kind to add much to what the first volume had shown.

INTRODUCTION

The picture of her relation to her sister was complete. But, in connection with other work, we have recently come across a great deal more of her correspondence, first at her old home at Broomhall, and secondly in Dean Stanley's papers, which were kindly lent to us by Lord Stanley of Alderley.

From sheer interest in the subject, without any intention of publication, we read these letters, and bit by bit a second volume shaped itself in our imagination – a volume of an entirely different type from the first, which was the picture of her early life as Lady Augusta Bruce. In this second volume, she emerges as Lady Augusta Stanley, living at Westminster, wife of the Dean and still the friend and confidante of the Queen.

The new volume does not profess to be a biography, but it is an attempt, by selection from her correspondence, to give a picture of her character in the new conditions, and to show the extraordinary width of her interests.

But again, I would insist that the object of our book is to reveal her character. Even her husband is incidental, and other events and people, in themselves of great interest, we have put on one side so as not to distract attention from the central figure. One cannot help being conscious that this book gives a slightly false impression of the later life of the Dean and Lady Augusta by dwelling predominantly on their journeys, their social life, and their relation with the Queen and the Royal Family. That is from the nature of the letters. The things of ordinary life did not strike her as of interest to her correspondents, and yet it was in those things that the greatness of her character and interests showed most clearly.

When Lady Augusta went to the Deanery the connec-

INTRODUCTION

tion with the Court and with the Royal Family was not broken. In some ways it became more important than the association of the earlier days. The whole series of the letters to the Queen, which were sanctioned for publication in connection with Dean Stanley's biography, show that she used her position outside the Court to bring before the Queen matters and points of view which would be denied to her in her more restricted surroundings at Windsor. In the same way she deliberately brought the Queen in touch with a great many of her subjects, either by what she wrote about them, or, as in the case of Carlyle, by arranging personal meetings at the Deanery, which would have been practically impossible elsewhere.

In spite of her passionate love of Scotland as her own home, she felt very strongly that the Queen, in her love for Scotland, was inclined to overlook other parts of her Empire, and especially Ireland. There was a continual effort in the letters to awaken an interest in Ireland, and to try to make the Queen feel the personal interest in Ireland that she felt in Scotland. This instance of the influence she tried to exercise is shown in the Irish letters in this volume.

She never wrote to the Queen about politics. She never tried to advocate causes, but the whole of the letters represent an intense desire to widen the Queen's sympathies towards every aspect of the lives of her subjects. With the younger members of the Royal Family, the same aim is obvious. For them she arranged dinners and meetings with interesting people, and she brought before them many sides of life which they also, but for her, might easily have overlooked.

She was acutely conscious that the death of the Prince

13

Consort had its evil consequences in shutting off the Royal Family from a great deal of the life of the country. Because she loved the Queen and the Royal children so much, she devoted herself to breaking down those barriers. Her influence was strengthened by her marriage, because of the confidence the Royal Family had in the Dean, and she was able to use that confidence to reinforce her own influence, in the direction of widening the Royal sympathies, and in clearing away misunderstandings.

The visit of the Dean and Lady Augusta to Russia has special interest, an interest to which we have felt it right to give a large space. The Russian chapters not only give an extremely interesting picture of the Russian Court in its glory, but the letters are all the more striking because she was never dazzled by the glory, nor lost her sense of the interest of the personal characters of the actors in the scene. Although the scenes in the Russian Court were so splendid, the Emperor and Empress, and all the others with whom she came in contact, are made very simple, natural, human people, in her letters.

The Russian visit has a pathetic interest to us now, because it was the cause of her illness and death. The prodigious number of letters, of which we publish perhaps a tenth part, were written at night, after tiring days, in which the strain of the climate, the state ceremonials and ponderous clothing exhausted a body which had long been overworked. When the collapse came, on their return to England, there was no vital force left to resist the power of illness.

I was only a boy at the time of my aunt's death, but I knew intimately, for many years, a great many of those who knew her best. What all people felt was that the interest which she shared with them must be the main and absorbing interest of her life. The clergy and workers among the poor of Westminster, could hardly believe that she had anything else than the events and interests of their lives to think of. Her work there seemed so complete, so all-absorbing. This was also true of the Westminster hospital and the development of nursing. She brought the same apparently undivided interest to all the family concerns of a wide circle of relations and friends. There is no doubt that one of the things which wore her out was her immense correspondence, which had to be carried on late into the night, when her days were so full. But in the correspondence these things which really occupied most of her life become incidental, the things which were more exceptional fill the biggest place.

I don't think that anyone can fail to be struck with the way in which she preserved the youthfulness of her mind, and the bubbling sense of humour, which remained undimmed by great sorrows, absorbing work, and an intense sense of the seriousness of life.

If she was intense and enthusiastic in connection with the concerns of the Queen, it was only the same intense-ness and enthusiasm which she gave to all these other interests. In the touching note at the end of this book, one sees that the reason for the esteem she inspired was the immense completeness of her love – a love which went out in earnest effort towards every one who came in contact with her. But that love was given pre-eminently to the husband of her choice. From the day she married him, though the link with her sister was never weakened, he became her central care, and she brought into his life just the qualities he needed. There was a childlike helplessness and simplicity about him in spite of his strength and his shrewdness, and he needed a practical mind to support and direct him. All her work was done in his library, at her writing-table, while he stood at his desk nearby and scattered the floor with endless papers. She was always ready when he wished to turn to her. She could always inspire him by the vividness of her interest in any work he was pursuing, and I can still see that same library, after her death, with her writing-table in its place, unused, her bust standing upon it, the very picture of the emptiness of life which her death brought to him. All the loving care that was given to him by others during the remaining years could not in any sense replace what she had been. The light had gone out of his life.

But beside this personal encouragement and support and care, she brought other things into his life. Her experience, both in Paris and at Court, had made her a perfect mistress of the *talent de société* in its highest form, a talent only seen at its best in an entirely unselfish person, and she brought this to bear upon his life. He was intensely interested in people and people were intensely interested in him. So she brought them together. Never has there been a house in London where such a variety of people were collected; it was not a house where people were collected simply because they were distinguished, but a house where brains brought brains, and interests brought interests. You would see statesmen and ecclesiastics, men of science, distinguished foreigners, poets, writers, people of position in the great world, indeed, almost every one who stood for anything in the life of England at that time. But, mixed with them, quite naturally and easily, some simple country clergyman or a woman from the nursing home or some parish worker, or just ordinary relations and friends. All were equally welcome, and all felt her extraordinary gift of bringing everybody into the circle.

She was herself always in the background. She always centred everything on him. It was only the commonplace people, or people who would have been left out, to whom she devoted herself personally. The result was a society of quite a unique character.

There were dinners and luncheons where she did carefully select the company, but, as a rule, the whole of the hospitality gave the feeling of being accidental. People were asked to lunch just because they called, or because they happened to be in London. Others dropped in casually, in the evenings. There was never any feeling of artificiality or arrangement. The evenings at the Deanery stand out most vividly in my memory. The Dean would stand near the tea table, drinking endless cups of tea, pouring out a conversation so vivid that it illuminated every subject he touched and drew in all those various intellectual forces. I can see him now. There would be Tyndal or Owen talking science. Kingsley or Bishop Temple or Bishop Wordsworth or some of his great antagonists in Convocation, like Archdeacon Denison, or Gladstone or Foster or any of the politicians. Renan might be the centre of one group and a Greek Archimandrite of another. Matthew Arnold and Locker would bring lightness and grace into the talk, or Carlyle pour out his fierce denunciations. Tennyson might stand, impressively and unquestionably, representing poetry, while Browning wandered round, deliberately inconspicuous as a man of the world. There came Jenny Lind, Christine Nilsson or Florence

Nightingale or Madame Mohl. I hardly ever see a name distinguished in the mid-nineteenth century without its recalling some scene at the Deanery, for those gatherings went on after her death, when I was older, though by then they had lost something of the life which she had given them.

The Dean's personality was vivid, childlike, and infinitely lovable. To me, as a little boy, and right on until his death, there was no interest like walking with him. In London, not a street was without its story. House after house had some quality or association to which he gave a vivid interest. And one was always meeting people and stopping to talk with them. I remember seeing old Carlyle on a bench on the Embankment and pausing while my uncle spoke with him. I remember meeting Dizzy, and the Dean's rather caustic comments as we left him.

But the remarkable circumstance in my memory is that one never thought of anybody as being distinguished. One thought of them as interesting. It never seemed unnatural or remarkable that they should be there. One took them for granted.

And side by side with such meetings were the almost weekly gatherings of working men whom he showed over the Abbey and to whom both Lady Augusta and the Dean gave exactly the same hospitality, the same vividness of interest that they showed to their distinguished visitors. There were, too, interesting occasions when distinguished foreigners came to the Deanery. Fortunately, the Dean possessed ample means, which made it possible for them to carry on this immense hospitality. But it was certainly used for the betterment of the world. People found inspiration in the width of his sympathies and in being brought into touch with countless people they would never otherwise have met. The Dean was a curious paradox in that he was the most excited of controversialists in public, but had in social intercourse the most supreme gift of bringing people of every kind and shade of opinion into personal sympathy. He was not a great theologian. Indeed, abstract thought was alien to his mind, yet abstract thinkers found him illuminating. He was not a scientist, and yet scientists loved to talk to him. He was not an accurate scholar, and yet he made scholarship live. He was a supreme historian, not because he wrote a great deal of first-rate history, but because, through his mind, history was translated to men into a living thing. Though he wrote nothing but a few verses, he was a poet, because life was poetry to him. And so scholars and poets, historians and politicians, scientists and philanthropists, found in him a focus of interest, and to this interest Lady Augusta ministered with the exquisite skill of her social tact.

There were amusing occasions, too. He was totally incapable of pretending, and to see him in the hands of a real bore was indescribably funny. He seemed to shrink up and settle down into a condition of pathetic helplessness. I can see him now, through a long lunch in which a man insisted on talking to him about nothing but racing. Once or twice in the letters there are allusions to this comicness of his appearance under such conditions.

He was one of those men to whom no one ever could suggest the faintest thought of coarseness. His biography shows the curious fact that through his whole time at Rugby, when there was a great deal of coarseness and evil there, even the crudest boys seemed to have shielded the purity of his mind. This is all the more remarkable, because he had a joyous sense of fun. Lady Augusta possessed joyousness too and a perfect sense of humour, but the background of their life was an intense and vital religion. Her half-sister, Lady Matilda Maxwell, wrote of her when she was ten years old:

'Augusta read much to me in Edinburgh. She prefers her Bible to her play in general, and I never have to choose for her. She has always some part selected for reading. She does not know where to find it, but she knows what it is about. "The woman whose sins were forgiven," and "She loved much," and "The young man who kept the commandments and yet lacked one thing."

'I asked her why she would always read about him.

'She looked up in a sort of reproachful way, "Oh, Jesus loved him! . . ." She seldom gets out of St. John. I never shall forget the expression with which she looked at me when the verse was read, "Behold the Lamb of God." I asked her afterwards why she gave me such a look. She said: "Was it not joy to hear our own favourite bit?"

'I gave her a large Bible in Edinburgh, and I thought her love for reading arose partly from the delight of such a *possession*. But she proposed parting with it, that I should take it home.

' "Papa may read it when he can't go to church, for the print is so large, and Mammy will like to read the Greek bits in the notes, and she will bring out all her Greek books, and cover the table with them, and then she will be happy."

'So she parted with her Bible, but not without a struggle. One day reading it, kneeling on the floor, and her large Bible on a chair, she kissed it very fervently and said: "Oh, Matty, I fear, I fear I can't be resigned to part with it." '

And that religious quality in her mind only expanded in later years.

But there is one thing, without which a picture of the Deanery would be incomplete. There were always children there. They both loved children. Nephews and nieces, the children of the other residents in the Cloisters, all kinds of children, found a home there, a home which they loved immensely. It was characteristic that the Dean walked in her funeral procession leading two children by the hand.

We hope that these letters may give a picture of the wonderful married years of her life, when she served the Queen, her husband and all those who came near her, with a love that was never sentimental, a kindly humour which was never critical and a wisdom which was never harsh or embittered. She left the world more glorious by her life and more empty by her death.

A. V. BAILLIE
Dean of Windsor

CHAPTER I

Lady Augusta Bruce becomes Lady Augusta
Stanley and goes to the Deanery at Westminster.
The Queen and employees at Woolwich. Bismarck
and Attila. Dean Stanley's character. Jenny Lind.
Swinburne and Mrs. Gaskell. Sir Frederick Bruce
in China. The Queen opens Parliament. Sir
Frederick Bruce in Washington. A visit to the
Queen of Holland. The Queen of Prussia's ques-
tions. Bishop Thirlwall of St. David's.

CHAPTER I

1864.

The first volume of Lady Augusta Stanley's letters ended when she was still Lady Augusta *Bruce*. In the last letter, written in November of 1863, she had nervously accepted Dean Stanley.

'It is *yes* that I have said, darling' (she wrote to her sister).
'I could not refuse, tho' he tried to frighten me!
'No one to be told till we hear from Windsor.
'Oh! my darling, it is like a dream.'

With the announcement of their engagement came the news that Dr. Stanley was to be the new Dean of Westminster. Lady Augusta had served the Duchess of Kent and the Queen for more than fourteen years. She had seen the aged Duchess fade, sadly and painfully, until she died, in the quiet of Frogmore.[1] She had supported the Queen in the death chamber of the Prince Consort and

[1] When the Duchess of Kent died, the Queen wrote to Lady Augusta: 'Dearest Augusta, – When you lost yr. dear Mother – now nearly a year ago, my beloved Mother whom God has taken to Himself and released from suffering, asked you to consider her House yr. Home henceforward – and I know that you mourn Her as yr. 2nd Mother! – I feel deeply yr. devotion to her and the tender, affectionate way in which you ministered to my dearest precious Mama. It is our wish that you should consider *our* house yr. home in future – I wish to appoint you my Resident Bedchamber Woman, and while I wish that you shd. live with us, I offer you the small apart. at St.

lived alone with Her Majesty in the sad days which followed. She was 'Guska' to the Princes and Princesses, and it was to her that Prince Arthur gave his heart when he was eight years old.

Princess Beatrice turned to her, a shocked child, to confess that she never thought 'there was stays in shops.' The older Princesses relied on her help and judgment, consulting her on all things, even when, like the Princess Royal, they married and made their homes away from England.

She was a denial of the Victorian tradition of false modesty and humourless hypocrisies. When, as a middle-aged woman, she married Dean Stanley, she was as joyous and gentle and wise as when she first came to the Duchess of Kent as a girl, from Paris, where she had lived with her mother, the Dowager Countess of Elgin. Her father, Thomas Lord Elgin, who brought the Marbles from the Parthenon, had died when she was quite young.

Filled with nervous concern about her own marriage, she was not beyond interest in other engagements of the same year. 'My darling, . . . I could dance the whole length of Regent Street,' she wrote to the Hon. Victoria Stuart-Wortley, who was to marry Mr. Welby about the same time.

The Queen was loath to lose her. At first she was against the union, for she did not believe that people with settled habits and independence should change their course of life

James' Palace in order that you may have a pied a terre of yr. own – Dearest Aa., the thought of having *you*, who dearest Mama loved as a Child, near me in future, is an indescribable comfort for my poor bleeding heart and I trust that you will love the Child of that dear blessed One who is at rest and at Peace now!'

26

by marrying in middle age. But she relented after a time, and when she called on them at the Deanery, Lady Augusta found that

'Nothing could be more touching and soothing than the beloved Queen's visit – so kind, so simple, so gentle and friendly. . . . The Queen came to my sitting-room and talked much, first of our sorrow and anxiety, then of the changes since I left her – much that went to my heart and overcame me greatly, but all in kindness. When we returned to the drawing-room she made us all sit down and Charlotte [her sister] greatly cheered her with some of her comical sayings. . . .'

She wrote to Dean Stanley, who was away at the moment:

'She spoke very kindly of you dearest, not a word of reproach. . . . The Queen wondered that she was not more struck by finding 2 of your photographs in my collection last summer, but I think that if I had not had a perfectly easy conscience, they would not have been there. She carried off one today. . . . I might go to Windsor on Monday when you return to Oxford – the beloved Queen's sympathy is most grateful to me.[1] I only dreaded the many faces I should have to see – but She said I might dine in my room.'

Lady Augusta had been closest and dearest of all friends during the bereavements of the Court. 'If it had not been for *you*, I really do not know how my Mother could have borne it,' the Prince of Wales had written to her after the Prince Consort's death. 'Pray always remain the same

[1] *Her brother, Lord Elgin, had just died while serving as Viceroy of India.*

to me, for what should I do without you my ever dear kind friend,' wrote Princess Helena, and Princess Beatrice, still a child, thought she would 'look very funny as *Deaness*,' and added, 'I suppose you are going to dress in a low white gown, or are you going to have a high white gown?'

The little Princess included the Dean in her affections and, after curds and sugar with him in the summer-house at Osborne, she beat him at croquet. 'It is very funny that you are going to be Dean of Westminster,' and equally *funny* she thought it that he was 'going to be married.'

She did not forget her tea party with the Dean. Very soon afterwards she offered Mrs. Bruce some cakes of her own making. Mrs. Bruce declined them.

'Very well then, as Dr. Stanley is not here, I shall give them to the donkey.'

So the *Deaness* in a *low white gown* did not leave an entirely gloomy and humourless Court to go first to Oxford and then to Westminster, as Lady Augusta Stanley. She wrote from Oxford, where Dr. Stanley was closing his brilliant career at Christ Church:

'I do not believe that I am Madame Stanley or that I am not the Resident Bed Chamber woman of 4 months ago.'

Her sister, Lady Frances Baillie, was still her confidante, and to her she admitted that she still felt

'very nervous of not doing and being all I shd. wish – very incapable of believing that he can care for me, and as he is just as nervous and incapable of expressing his feelings, it is slightly a vicious circle. Still I find all so

28

much easier – his gentleness and simplicity and indulgence so disarming to one's shyness and sense of inferiority, that I begin to feel as if some day I might almost count upon him as I do on you. The House is so quiet and homelike, so like old houses I remember in my youth – everything is so quiet, so methodical, so gentlemanlike, that I feel as if I had only gone back some years and taken up the old thread of my life.

'We have been twice at early Church, but in general have prayers only at nine and breakfast after. Then Church at 10 or not and we write or occupy ourselves till luncheon at one – at 2. we walk or drive, today to where Amy Robsart was murdered, – come home at 4 or 5 if we go to Service, tea and a quiet time till dinner – I do not sit in my room at all – it looks quite English with the window wide open all day. All manner of beautiful tidy arrangts. planned by V. and carried out by Mawley – night things in a muslin, lined with pink – pincushions – muslin covers – my lovely brushes. . . . This room is so pretty – light green walls, white and gold cornice-oak doors – a few prints and drawings – oak book case – round table seat – comfy chairs – two windows looking on garden – dining room below and windows, etc. – my room above looks out on Ch. Ch. Quadrangle.

'Miss Stanley [the Dean's sister] and [Canon] "Hugh Pearson," [1] come down on the 4th and we go to London on 8th – to Edinboro' on the 16th, perhaps before.'

The story of Lady Augusta's life at the Deanery and in the terms when she resumed her position in the Victorian

---

[1] With whom Dean Stanley maintained a constant friendship and correspondence until his death.

Court is told in the letters she continued to write to her sister.

March 17.

The Christening of the Duke of Clarence was beautiful and affecting. – The Queen looked so handsome and graceful – people, so thankful, came for this reappearance – She *evidently* unconscious, took pleasure in it Herself. So loving and kind to me – He and I went down yesty. and met Her at Frogmore [1] – so beautiful and bright – so full of memories, loving and unspeakably grateful – Oh! darling how it took me back, and how I longed for you. – I am very glad not to sever my connections with those dear Ones – only at this moment it is trying to leave for a month.

— came to the station with us yesdy. and [her young daughter] ran up for a penny to buy *Fun.* Uncle A. [Dean Stanley] highly disapproves of such literature for the young. Poor Lamb, her ways are most sad. The other day in a shop I found her looking up in the face of a Shopman, with the most *awful* chaffing expression, really a sort of bad woman look – poor lamb, so impudent was she in her innocence.

May 6th.

. . . Wedy. a lovely dinner at Marlboro' House. The Master and Mistress [the Prince and Princess of Wales] charming, and all as nice as possible. . . . I know that the Queen never heads sub: lists for private purposes and that She cannot, I fear, make an exception in favour of Mrs. W. Her private pension list is more than full and there are some heart-rending appeals every day. A

[1] The house in the Home Park at Windsor, where Lady Augusta had lived for many years as Lady-in-Waiting to the Duchess of Kent.

subscription would be the only thing, I feel assured, and when one sees how money is subscribed for fooleries, one is vexed that it should be so difficult to obtain for such cases.

Monday, Dec. 12.

There is to be a sort of service on the 14th at the Mausoleum, [at Frogmore] which we all deprecate – pour comble de malheur, the Dean is ill and has asked my Dean!!! if he does it, it must be published. Why?

Friday, 17.

Found yr. dear note of the 14th on our return from dining with Earl Russell[1] last night – that funny Lady Louisa Howard, Ly. Fanny's Sister in law, Ld. Lansdowne's daughter was there, very nice. – Layard told us a good thing, that in Paris instead of saying now 'vous m'embêtez' you say 'vous m'encycliquez.' – Is it not good? . . .

Prothero, the Dean's biographer, writes an interesting description of the early relations between the Dean, Lady Augusta and the Chapter at Westminster. 'He was on good terms with every member of the Chapter, and Dr. Wordsworth [who had opposed his appointment] became his warmest friend. This peaceful entrance upon his office Stanley owed partly to his own resolve of keeping silent under all attacks, partly to the conciliatory tact of his wife, who spared no pains to smooth his path.

'Is it possible,' asked one of the canons, who was struck by the cordial warmth of her manner, 'that all this can be sincere?'

'Yes,' was the reply of the Duchess of Buccleuch; 'it is the echo of her heart.' Every day Stanley learned to lean more and more upon his wife.

[1] *The Lord John Russell of the Reform Bill.*

Lady Augusta's sister-in-law, the Hon. Mrs. Robert Bruce, had been appointed to be one of the Queen's Ladies. Some months before the events in the above letters, she wrote to Dr. Stanley:

'As no contradiction has appeared in *The Times* to the paragraph in Monday's paper, stating that people employed at Woolwich were to be arrested if they looked out of windows at the Queen as she passed etc., I hope you will take every opportunity of saying that any such absurd orders were quite against H.M.'s wishes. When I glanced at the *The Times* on my arrival on Monday, from Osborne, I saw the paragraph and took the first opportunity of asking H.M. if she had noticed it. She told me She had and had sent Prince Alfred to tell General Grey how indignant She was and desired him to enquire into the matter. He went to the War Office and created a great commotion, but unluckily was over persuaded not to send the denial he had himself written to the Papers. During my afternoon in London and on my arrival here I found people so furious with the Queen that I am quite unhappy about it and have taken measures to have the story contradicted in the Scotch papers. The Queen was pretty well when I left her. Prince Leopold rather lame. Princess Beatrice in great force. She has at last begun her long delayed writing lessons, but struck work the other day after making a line of the letter P. "It is so difficult to make their stomachs." Not a bad idea. . . . H.M. had Morning prayers last Sunday instead of Litany and Sermon "because I was so hot." You can fancy Her wrath when She discovered how long both Lessons and the Psalms were on that day.'

32

Lady Augusta Stanley left the Deanery at intervals, and resumed her place at Court. She and the Dean wrote daily. He consulted her about his sermons, because he could not 'throw himself' into them unless he knew 'that they have your approval beforehand.' He hoped that her 'thoughts turn back to this dear library and that you are here in heart and spirit.' He read 'the Lessons in the Abbey' and told her that the 'fine Chapter of Deuteronomy was almost as good as a sermon. I only wish the eagle would have stopped his neck [he was so small that he was hidden behind the lectern] a little, so as not to have thrust up his head between me and the congregation.'

In August of 1864 they went to the Continent, staying first of all in French country houses. From Berne, Lady Augusta wrote to the Queen:

'Saw Prince Arthur [1] this morning [having arrived last night]. We met H.R.H. at the door of the English Church. . . . I cannot express the pleasure it gave us to see such healthful looks and good spirits. H.R.H. has grown and has a robust air – in every way one sees that the exertions made and the feats accomplished have agreed. . . . H.R.H.'s animated account of the expeditions interested us much and put to shame our leisurely and very humble proceedings. . . .'

Later in the year she wrote to the Queen:

'I must tell Your Majesty that I was startled in the Abbey today by a plagiarism in the Dean's sermon – no other than Your Majesty's definition of the true church (in answer to the Prince of Wales) which he had permitted himself to adopt.'

[1] The Duke of Connaught.

During one of her first visits to Osborne, after her marriage, she wrote to her sister:

'A year ago Bismarck told the Minister from Wurtemburg that the plan urged on Prussia as giving her all the real influence she could require without alienating the Smaller Powers – viz. that of accepting the Military and Naval Supremacy in the Duchies, which none would contest, while avoiding annexation, would not suit the King – but, said the Minister, H.M. is open to conviction, and would be persuaded by you.

' "But I could not urge such a policy," replied B., "for something more striking, more to be remembered is essential to the firm establishment of *my position*. I owe it to myself."

'Lately he argued in the same strain with Ld. A. Loftus and pointed out to him how much greater a man Attila was than your John Bright, and how much more the D. of Wellington will be remembered by his campaigns than by his statesmanship!!!

'Is that not wonderful? Only imagine a man putting forth such sentiments – and arguing how trifling a consideration the fall of a few thousand men in battle was, compared with the carrying out of some great political scheme, for the establishment of his position! Genl. Grey was so much amused by the "rapprochement" of Attila and J. Bright. He says that Ld. A. Loftus' despatches have been very good at this juncture, better than Ld. Napier's which are always lengthy and wordy in the extreme. He quite appreciates the superiority of Napier as a companion . . . but the Despatches of the latter are superior. How strange that is! . . .'

34

Both the Dean and Lady Augusta entered upon a life of unrelenting duties when they returned to the Deanery at Westminster. Their life is the story of the gradual merging of two great characters and spirits into a unity which became a tremendous influence for good and a power for charity and right thinking, right up to the time of Lady Augusta's death. A glow of spiritual inspiration enriches all that happened at Westminster in the years that followed their marriage, an inspiration all the more lovely because it was personal and not without humour and pleasure for both of them.

Dean Stanley was so clear cut and different from any of his contemporaries that the story of his habits may make him seem almost eccentric, but his little characteristic differences proceeded from a gentle helplessness, a detached, almost ethereal character which was confused and inadequate when he was faced with mundane occupations. Yet he was practical in his work and, although his material helplessness may have suggested the character of a dreamer, he was never vague in dealing with people or occasions.[1]

The Dean's biographer gives a picture of breakfast at the Deanery. 'At nine o'clock . . . a meal over which

---

[1] That the Dean was able to cope with a situation with precision and humour was shown some years later when a madman was brought into the Library at Westminster. He approached the Dean and, in threatening tones, he said: 'Mr. Dean, I have a message to you from God. You are to take me to the Queen, whom I am to address on a most solemn matter.'

'In that case,' said the Dean, 'there is not a moment to lose.'

Opening the door, he ushered the visitor downstairs, through the hall, picking up his hat on the way. When they reached the front door Dean Stanley opened it, passed the visitor out and then closed it between them.

he liked to linger when he had interesting guests staying in the house. But he ate scarcely anything himself. A hard-boiled egg, from which his wife had peeled the shell, two slices of toast, buttered and cut into small pieces, and tea satisfied his appetite. . . . At 10.30 he entered the library with the letters of the day, or more often left a trail of papers behind him which had to be gathered up by his wife or his secretary.'

He was so helpless that he could not dress himself. Buttons were the bane of his life and they were inevitably done up into the wrong buttonhole. He never wore gaiters because of the buttons they entailed, and his collar and tie had a habit of separating. He would look pathetic if you pointed out these little shortcomings to him. He had no sense of taste or smell, a fact which intrigued Princess Beatrice so much that, when he first met her in the corridor at Windsor, 'She was with Mrs. Bruce, and when I came up to them there was much whispering and entreaty. She wished Mrs. Bruce to ask a question which she was at last induced to put herself. "Is it true that he can neither taste nor smell?" Then followed an animated conversation on tasting and smelling.'

He always stood at his desk when he was writing, in the same room where Lady Augusta worked, at her table.

'We sit in the Library,' she writes. 'A. stands at his desk in the little closet off the room where he can be as untidy as he likes!!!!

'We have been correcting the Proofs of the Sermon of the 28th tonight. So funny to me to be asked words. I, who never know any for my own use, and to find that the gentle loving confiding spirit which the Being at the desk

36

breathes makes me find them quite naturally – just like when my own darling speaks with me – then all sorts of odds and ends that I never dreamed of, find themselves at the bottom, and available.'

Feb. 16, 1865.

'The other day John appeared before Luncheon, pale with horror – "The P. of Wales is in the Drawingroom." My toilet was mild and my first idea was that there was probably no fire, but luckily that was not the case. – He was so nice. . . . We have had daily 30 to lunch for Convocation, since Tuesday. It goes on tomorrow also.

'One evening Jenny Lind came and sang "Auld Robin Gray" – quite beautiful – the pathos of "Auld Robin Gray," the variety and depth of feeling and expression she put into it were quite wonderful. A. received the guests and got so enthusiastic at last, that he declared to Jenny that he began to see the difference!!! Such a triumph.'

That the Dean should 'see the difference' between one song and another was indeed a triumph, for he had no ear for music, and the only piece he ever recognised was the 'Dead March in Saul,' because of the drums. If the drums were left out, he was furious, because he could not recognise it. If they had been introduced into 'God save the King,' he would have thought he was listening to the Dead March.

But the way of life at the Deanery was not always smooth. In one letter, Lady Augusta says:

'Did I tell you that I was at a meeting when A. was coughed down and hissed. He never moved and I found it easier to bear than I expected and was only a little

LATER LETTERS OF LADY A. STANLEY

tempted to poke some of the voters near me with my parasol. Catherine Vaughan [Dean Stanley's sister] says she would have laid about her right and left!' Mrs. Vaughan's friendship was a source of pleasure to Lady Augusta. Her presence when in London and her letters when she was away both lent colour to the life at Westminster. A fragment of one of her letters is preserved among Lady Augusta's papers, written after she had

'spent two days at Lord Houghton's – where we met Mr. and Mrs. Maurice, Mrs.[1] *and Miss Gaskell,* Mr. and Mrs. Robert Lowe, Reginald Cholmondeley and my old enemy, the Poet Swinburne. I was so delighted to see Mrs. Gaskell and to talk to her about my darling Augusta.

'What a contrast, she in her retiring modesty – presented to the horrid little Swinburne, who is now so inflated with his fame, that he is hardly bearable.

'Only think of the aggravation – I am dying to hear Maurice and Mrs. Gaskell talk – Instead of this, we were condemned to sit in a solemn circle, and hear this rising genius declaim his New Tragedy of "Mary Queen of Scots." It took 4 hours to read and a more improper production I never heard. It was *so* improper, that we none of us knew wh. way to look!'

Lady Augusta's brother, Sir Frederick Bruce, was British Minister in Pekin, and she had to include Chinese affairs among her interests, for she received a constant stream of letters from him. About the time of her marriage, he wrote:

'By way of variety I have the Danish Minister and a Prince Wittgenstein as my guests – the latter since

[1] Author of *Cranford* and the *Life of Charlotte Brontë.*

38

February. I have had a very pleasant shooting trip of twenty days to Mongolia, and enjoyed antelope stalking on Mongolian ponies, and various kinds of shooting. It has done me a great deal good and stirred up my liver, I hope, for summer wear – Nothing could be so civil and friendly as the population of this neighbourhood. One can do anything with a joke, and I know Chinese enough to make bad ones which produce a very wholesome effect.

Later.

'I have the Danish Minister as my guest for three months & I am glad to say that he has at last obtained an excellent Treaty – The late alliance stood me in good stead with the Chinese, upon whom I did not fail to impress the interest we took in his success.

'. . . I am afraid we are in for a row with Japan – we shall not escape from this domination as long as our Govt. does not insist on our people behaving with more discretion in these Eastern countries. Non-official people in Japan are obliged to get out of the way of a Damio [Japanese Noble] or to dismount when he passes and a party ought to have turned back when they saw him approaching. These rows always happen to our people, whose ideas are perverted by India and treat these nations as if they are conquered. I am afraid that the Govt. will find a Japanese war a more serious enterprise than they have been made to believe by [Sir Rutherford] Alcock.'

In June of the following year, 1864, he wrote:

'I hope to get away from here in May. . . . Five years of the China task is as much as anyone ought to be called on to endure, and during that period I have not been a day out of harness. I expect to find Europe in a lively state at the time I reach it. Our friend L.[ord] Napier seems bent on excelling the fame of Don Quixote. I trust we shall let him fight his windmills alone in future and not embark on diplomatic or other enterprises with him. John Bull is not fitted for such tricks – he is awkward when he tries to dance the French jig. . . . I am getting on well as far as I can judge. My great object is to act in the spirit of a "gentleman" to this Govt. that is, to treat them with courtesy, to admit and respect their rights, and in all matters as much as possible to "save their faces," which is everything to a Gov. proud, not unreasonably, of being at the head of this great civilisation, and which is very sensitive on the point of dignity, as it governs chiefly by moral influence, not force. . . . Govs. and nations are the same as individuals – tact and real courtesy [not the external sham] are just as necessary to produce friendship between nations as between men. . . . When you see Gladstone, give him my best regards and read to him what I have said above. . . . There is no reason why we should not gain their confidence sufficiently to enable us to trade in peace now we are at Pekin alongside of the Government and able to explain what we are and what we intend. But let him beware of charlatans and impostors of men who talk of railways and telegraphs, as of projects which must at all hazards be forced down the throats of the Chinese – I do not at all despair of the Chinese gradually adopting such improvements, for they are intelligent and not averse to material improvements, whenever they see the benefit, and can undertake them, without danger to their political fabric. But these changes will only be a source of danger to our relations if they are *exotics* and not the spontaneous products of Chinese enlightenment. Our task is that of the schoolmaster who educates, not of the tyrant who imposes. . . . I don't think that it would do any harm if Lord Russell were to hear this letter – dropping out the allusion to Gladstone.'

The Queen opened Parliament in 1865, coming out from her retirement, returning to Osborne, 'much exhausted.' Lady Augusta wrote to her sister:

My own darling,

All I hear is most satisfactory. Our Press informant said yesty. that people were pleased and satisfied. – The impression had been good and that now, if only the Q. would keep up the confidence and good feeling, which wd. be comparatively easy, She would be as popular as ever – A. had remarked how much more enthusiastic the cheering for the Wales couple had been, than that for Her – but this was accounted for by the awkwardness of the mixed feelings of joy and sympathy, and our important informant said the P. of W. is like one given credit to, for what he *will* do. But he has his spurs to win. Whereas his Mother has only to be worthy of her own past . . . to keep up Her position and influence in the Country and society. I felt so unable to rejoice as much as I should have done, not knowing at all Her own impressions of those without, but from a letter from Prss. H[elen]a today which I shall forward I hope, She was softened and gratified and in a good frame. . . . All say she looked grave, but bowed kindly and unceasingly on all sides, and sat forward as one would have wished. Dress very handsome and becoming, the robes looked handsome, tho' of course the Pages etc. were a grt. loss. – The scene was splendid – the House crowded in every corner.

Feb: 1865.

I do hope that the reception was good – in some places unkind things were said and some one told – that she had heard a man in the crowd say while waiting 'If she does not bow I'll strike her' – but when the cortege appeared and She did bow, the whole was swallowed up in enthusiasm. This is very interesting and important, if true, and I believe that it is and that it represents the condition of much public feeling before, and the effect of Her appearance. My first impressions were from K., who was outside . . . and heard the merry cheering for the Young Couple and the more solemn reception of H.M.

Lady Augusta's brother, Sir Frederick Bruce, was now British Minister in Washington and her interests were extended to include American affairs, for his letters were frequent and interesting. In May of 1865, he wrote:

'Everyone is taken up with the trials and with the evidence adduced, showing the bitterness of the passions evoked by this civil war. . . . There seems little doubt that [plans?] for burning cities, vessels, etc., were adopted by the Southern leaders. The Northerners will call them savages and no doubt the fact of living among slaves does tend to make men intolerable barbarians – but they only try to retaliate in the north what they suffered at the hands of the Federal Generals and troops and exasperated as they were, I can understand any case of revenge – but nothing has come out to implicate Davies in assassination – no civil war was ever attended with such ruin and humiliation to the defeated and there exists upon earth no race more violent and unscrupulous than the men of the south.

You can fancy what a prospect it is – with 4,000,000 of suddenly emancipated Blacks.

'I trust the King of the Belgians is better. He would be a sad loss to Europe and to the Queen in particular. I fear his Mexican daughter is likely to have a very unpleasing time.'

Later he wrote:

'I hope people in England do not delude themselves with the idea that their difficulties in this country are over. Mexico and reconstruction have kept them tolerably quiet and the latter check may exist for some time – but sooner or later we shall have serious consequences if we cannot hit on a more amiable way of settling points at issue, than we have adopted hitherto.'

In August of 1865, the Dean and Lady Augusta left England for their holiday together. Their first host was the Queen of Holland. 'God bless and keep you both! Do not forget me. My friendship is real and from my whole heart, and I trust I shall ever find you equally kind and true to me,' Queen Sophia had written to Lady Augusta. From Holland, where the Dean found the Queen's consideration and intelligence 'for her position, very remarkable,' they went to stay with Lady Frances Baillie and her husband, who was British Chargé d'Affaires at Baden. They went

'to tea with the Princess Hohenlohe, the Queen of Prussia, alone, coming in the evening. The Queen in public is very stately, full of set phrases. But on this occasion she sat down, and poured forth a continuous flow of questions to me to be answered, listening very attentively to me till

I had finished my answer, and then beginning a new question.

'These are some of the questions: – (1) How old is the world? (2) What is the oldest portion of the human race? (3) What difference is there between the Jews in Palestine and the Jews in Europe, and do they retain their ancient usages? (4) Are there any likenesses between the Jewish religion and the Egyptian? . . . Each of these questions, stated at length and with much precision, certainly gave me a considerable notion of her knowledge and intelligence. . . .'

They went to Venice, Italy, Switzerland, and France, and in October they returned to England and closed their holiday with a visit to Bishop Thirlwall of St. David's, the Historian. The Dean found it

'charming to see him surrounded by his books of every kind, and always with one of them in his hands, going every evening to feed his swans and ducks in the pond at the bottom of the garden,'

and Lady Augusta resumed her letters to the sister with whom she had stayed in Baden, writing from the Bishop's Palace:

'Came here Wedy. – nice place, pretty country and a wonderfully wise old poet, a perfect mine of learning – there is nothing he does not know and he lives in his books – an old Bachelor – but so nice and tender and good, under a cold exterior. It is charming to hear him converse and to ask him anything. . . .'

CHAPTER II

Dean Stanley on Marriage. Princess Beatrice and
Lot's wife. Jowett and Lady Augusta. Letters from
Princess Helena: her Marriage. Vallombrosa.
Avignon. Toulouse. Mr. Gladstone in Rome. The
Dean, the Pope, and the Queen.

Dean Stanley had expressed his feelings about marriage in an earlier letter to Lady Augusta:

'. . . a dim mysterious feeling, as of gradually drawing nearer to the confines of a new world. I have often thought, and I remember telling the Queen, in speaking of the marriage of the Prince of Wales, that Marriage was the only event in modern life which corresponds to what Baptism was in the ancient Church – a second birth, a new creation, old things passing away, all things becoming new. . . . You must be my wings. I shall often flag and be dispirited; but you, now, as my dear mother formerly, must urge me on, and bid me not despair when the world seems too heavy a burden to be struggled against.'

Their marriage fulfilled this hope. Prothero writes:

'He drew fresh vigour from the companionship of a wife who made herself one with him to an extraordinary degree . . . strong in her self-control, no passionate or unguarded word ever escaped her lips. Admitted, as she was, to the most intimate confidence of the Queen, she showed a devotion to her Royal Mistress and friend which was not less remarkable for its silence than for its fidelity.'

But the association of the Queen and Court with the

life at the Deanery was not without humour. Princess Beatrice was still young enough to ask lively and guileless questions, and just as she had adopted Lady Augusta for her friend so she elected the Dean to be her religious adviser. The Hon. Mrs. Bruce wrote to the Dean:

'H.M. has just left my room, and was talking of the sermon on Whitsunday which she had been reading this morning, as having made a great impression on Her –

'I have another request to make to you and this time from Pss. Beatrice. The History of Lot and his wife was read to her yesterday and she was much taken up about the fate of the "poor lady." Today, when she was having her dinner at the Queen's luncheon table, and some salt on her plate – she exclaimed, perhaps that is a bit of Lot's wife – the little Pss. entered into a long discussion as to the kind of salt into which Lot's wife was turned – whether it really was like what was in the salt cellars, that the Queen at last said, "Well, suppose you ask Bertie – he has been at the Dead Sea, you know" –

' "No," the child answered, "Bertie could not know, I shall ask Mrs. Bruce to write to Mr. Stanley and ask him." – She came in accordingly and asked me to write to you – and has twice since run in to know whether I have done so – If you will send her a message about it, you will cause great delight. . . .'

She wrote to 'The Reverant Lady Augusta Stanley,' and hoped she would 'come to lunshen,' and then:

'Dearest, I hope you are not annoyed with my letters dear, but do not mind answering them dear. . . . I am going to make this letter very long dear. I am going to have my tooth pulled out tomorro.'

48

And then, a little unsympathetically:

'Dear Mama has a headache. We are very happy dear.'

With all his helplessness and childlike qualities, his gentleness, Dean Stanley was a firebrand when there was a losing cause to be championed. He 'lived in an atmosphere of contention which thickened rather than dispersed in the course of years.' Bishop Colenso's heresy might have been less than a nine days' wonder if it were not for the fact that Dean Stanley raised his voice in defence of the Bishop of Natal. In other Church matters, too, his enthusiasms were dramatic and his opinions forcibly expressed. Parallel with his 'atmosphere of contention' at Westminster came his increasing favour in the eyes of the Queen. And he had a third interest in retaining his friends at Oxford. He maintained a spirited correspondence with Canon Pearson, Bunsen, the Prussian Ambassador, and Professor Jowett, who wrote of Lady Augusta: 'I saw the lady once, and I thought she was frank and good and wise, and very unlike my imperfect notions of people who live at Court, in being the most natural person in the world.' Jowett had resented and deplored his removal from Oxford.

'Will you let me tell you my mind about this, that if possible, Dr. Stanley may be induced to reconsider his decision. One of our theological opponents appears to me to have a true insight on this subject. He says Lord Palmerston has done quite right in removing him from a place in which he was doing great mischief to one in which he will be comparatively innocuous. . . . I fully recognise the claims which the Queen has upon him, but I am sure

49   D

that he can only serve the Queen really (excuse the paradox) by being independent of her wishes.'

The Dean had increased his circle to include Lady Augusta's family and friends. Among these was Frederick Locker, the poet and critic, who had married Lady Augusta's sister Charlotte. There are still many people who treasure his *London Lyrics*. Apropos of the Dean's total inability to appreciate 'the difference between eighteen pence and one-and-eightpence,' Frederick Locker left an amusing story:

'I was telling him that musician Halle's cook had lately won a good round sum of money in a lottery with the number 23. Halle was interested, and asked her how she came to fix on so lucky a number. "Oh! Sir," said she, "I had a dream. I dreamt of seven three times, and as three times seven makes twenty-three, I chose that number, Sir."'

When Locker finished the story, he observed a wistful expression on Arthur's countenance, as if he were ready, nay, anxious to be amused, but could not for the life of him quite manage it.

Then suddenly his face brightened, and he said, but not without a tinge of dejection, 'Ah, yes, I see; yes, I suppose three times seven is *not* twenty-three.'

His mathematics and difficulties with money calculations were notorious; also his handwriting which once inspired an unofficial deputation of protest from the Post Office.[1]

[1] On one occasion he wrote on business to a tradesman whose reply was long delayed. At last the answer came: 'Not being acquainted,' wrote the tradesman, 'with the caligraphy of the higher orders, I asked a friend to decipher parts of the note.'

In January, Princess Helena had written to her:

Dearest Augusta,

Mama hopes you could come on the 1st April till the 1st May, during that time we often hope to see his Reverence at Windsor. . . . Now I have another question to ask. My Prince is very anxious to read a good book about the English Church, where the difference between High and Low Church are explained – He asked me if I knew any book, I said I did not, but would write to you who would be sure to know of one, at least His Reverence would, also could you name a good history of England. The Prince has read Macaulay's History but he is anxious to study it (History) a little more – I am very troublesome I fear, but Dear 'Guska' will forgive if I teaze her –

Later, in February, Princess Helena wrote:

Dearest Augusta,

Mama desires me to write you these lines in her name –

Mama is anxious if there is not *actual* bar against it to give me away at my wedding –

At the time of Alice's marriage there was a question of it, and I believe then the Dean of Windsor thought it might be done, *then* Mama did not wish to do it –

Mama will walk with me to the Altar on that eventful day and is anxious to give me away – She says as she is the Sovereign and does the work of man and is in a peculiar position now, that she does not see why she cd. not do it as well as she sits on a throne and does so many things wh. a man does, why she cd. not do this also – Will you ask his Reverence about it, and whether there is any bar that prevents it.

I fear my explanation is not very clear. . . .

After the wedding she wrote again to Lady Augusta:

. . . It was a great pleasure to receive your dear letter this morning, and I hasten to thank you for it – My dear Mama was quite wonderful on Tuesday, at the opening of Parliament and there was such a lovely expression on her dear face as she bowed her thanks to her subjects who all along the road cheered and welcomed her – It did one's heart good to see the delight, the joy of all around at seeing her again. But it was a fearful trial for Mama, yet she was wonderfully calm. – I thought she looked too beautiful sitting on her throne. – She did not feel so tired at first, but today she is much exhausted . . . and very nervous, yet so loving and dear – She must have some little time complete quiet now – She is not ill, but much shaken – You can think how I trembled for her on that day, how I longed to be able to help her more. She was much touched by the affection all showed her. – Thanks darling for your kind wishes, that I was nervous when my name was read out coupled with the name of that beloved one you will not be astonished at, yet I felt so proud so happy and when my eyes met his, you will easily think what passed in our minds, such deep gratitude for our great happiness. The separation was dreadful and I cannot speak of it – He will be back on the 30th of April, wh. seems an age to me – I am intensely happy – what he is I cannot find words to say, so noble, generous, loving and such tact and discretion, never shrinking fr. saying what he thinks right – To *you* I say all this what I would not do to others. – I cannot say *how* happy I am – God has indeed richly blessed me and my heart is filled with gratitude. Dear Christian is at Brussels today and will be at Kiel on Saturday in the middle of the day – *How* I miss him I *cannot* say – He has been such a help and comfort to me these last weeks for I have had very much to do and many worries in relation to the Ceremony of Tuesday – But still they were quiet very happy weeks, the 3 we passed together, and it would be very wrong of me to fret at his departure. I have not yet thanked you for your letter I received on Tuesday at Windsor. . . .

I have written you such an untidy letter, forgive me. I am very tired and my thoughts with him.

God bless you.

Your loving,

HELENA.

In the autumn of 1866, they went to France and then to Florence and Rome. The Dean was not interested in scenery in the abstract. But any place with historical associations or the site of a dramatic event enthralled him. Nor was he interested in art galleries, and Lady Augusta reported from Florence that he was 'rather low at the prospect of five days in this city of pictures, but got over it better than he expected.'

She wrote to her sister of Vallombrosa:

'Here is the spot from which a letter must be begun to you – Here are "the autumnal leaves that strew the brooks in Vallombrosa, where the Etruscan shades, high overarched embower" – Do you not think that Milton's visit to Florence is one of the most poetical incidents of his life? Here and there, he met the blind old Galileo suffering from the effects of the "Inquisition," "The Tuscan artist who from the top of Fiesole" explored the Moon – himself before he wrote these lines to become blind also? And then it was that he made that same journey to Vallombrosa which we have now made, and of which the recollection must have been treasured up in his mind, thro' all the thirty years of civil wars and poverty, and blindness, till it came out in these verses which are, as you shall hear as exact as if he had written them on the spot today – It was as with him, on "an autumnal" day that the peasants on one of the "Etruscan mountains" who were feeding Gurthwise their swine under the shade of the chestnut trees, or beating down the chestnuts from the spreading branches – saw a man and woman walking up the stony path, which now as doubtless in Milton's time leads from the foot of the hills to the Convent – These two were yr. Cousins A. and A.

'We left our carriage at the Village of Tosi and made this delightful walk of two hours in the cool of a beautiful evening – every feature of the scene agrees – The "Etruscan shades" which give their name to the "Valley of Shades" – "Vallis Umbrosa" – are first wide glades of chestnuts – succeeded by a dark belt of pines, above which again, crowning the crest of the hills, warm and purple with the tints of Autumn, is a forest of beech – The "leaves" are chiefly from the chestnuts "strewn" about in every direction, not merely from the October winds but from the havoc of the chestnut gatherers, of whom I have just spoken. They are "strewn" on the "brooks": – This is an essential characteristic of the place – Indeed its first name was "Acqua Bella." The Springs and rivulets burst forth in every little glen – falling in cascades whose

54

murmurs must have murmured in Milton's ears as it did
in ours – And down on their clear rills and polished stones
were showered the falling leaves, from right and left.
"High overarched" and most "deeply entwined" are the
tall pines – shooting up like the columns of endless naves
and transepts – and thro' these we reached the Convent
which lies just between them and the purple lines of
beeches. As you look from Florence you can just see a
white spot like a star in the night, gleaming from the dark
bosom of the mountain, that is the upper Convent, "the
Saradisine" as it is called – perched on a craggy rock and
overlooking the whole plain of the Arno, the dome of
Florence Cathedral just visible and the range of the
Carara Hills rising beyond. The lower and larger Convent is a large modern building of the date of 1627. This
or 1628 is the very date of Milton's visit – He must have
arrived just at the moment of its completion, and slept in
the very apartments still used for travellers – Some kind
soul has put there in memory of him, a photograph of the
fallen angels in Paradise Lost.

'But alas! for Vallombrosa! It was a melancholy day
for the poor Monks when we arrived. It was the last day
of their possession – as we toiled up to the last ascent thro'
the pine forest we met a cavalcade coming down the hill
– a grave dignitary in front on horseback; others, some
on horses – some drawn in baskets by huge white oxen.
These as we heard on reaching the Convent, were the
Prior and the Govt. Officers, to whom he had just made
over the keys and the title deeds of the Monastery, and we
found only 4 or 5 left to take charge of the buildings for
the next few weeks before their final departure – They
were sadly cast down – Some had had been there 20 and

30 years and now have to retire on their little pensions and leave their beautiful haunts – It quite grieved our hearts to see and think of them: so departed, I suppose, the Monks of Glastonbury and West. 300 years ago – but West. has still remained with something worthy of its great name – while Vallombrosa will in a few years be nothing but a name. – I could not help thinking whether our turn would ever come again and West. also be a desert – "Light be the hand of ruin laid." Still I must confess that in my heart of hearts I felt it difficult to say aught against the suppression of Vallombrosa – It gave me quite a different impression from Monte Cassino – There all was life, action, intelligence, usefulness, besides the great unbroken series of historical recollections – Here, tho' the good Monks were very kind, they were very dull – they had nothing to say and nothing to do – except shoot in the woods and keep the farms. There was no one to teach, unless they went down to the Village at the foot of the mountain, from which in the winter the snow cuts them off. When I asked for a history of the Monastery they had none except an account of the Life of the Founder: whether because they did not care to possess one or because their annals are so vacant that it has no history, I do not know – So that I do not know after all, which was most sad, – that such a long association should at last be severed, or that such a venerable Institution should have lasted so long and done so little – Travellers no doubt will miss them – the accommodation was very comfortable and was all that can be had there. We were alone in the lodgings where Ladies are admitted, and were well provided.

'In the morning we strayed over the Hills and saw

Florence stretched beneath us, and then with the help first of a stupid Monk and then of a very vivacious Gardener, I tracked out the legendary sites of the Founder's history – They are all full of "leaves" and "brooks" as they ought to be. – "John Gualtiro," in 1015 forgave his Brother's murderer on Good Friday and came off into the mountains – First he arrived at a Spring – "Virtuosa Acqua" as Benedetto assured us for all the pains of the body – Then he thought himself not enough secluded and took up his post under a beech, which spread its branches and put out its foliage to receive him – (excellent charm, these leaves, says Benedetto, against lightning!) In the Church is *his arm* (for he was buried elsewhere when he died) – which was twice taken by the Florentines to Sta. Maria Novella and brought back by Angels – a great event celebrated July 12 – On a rock under the Church is a sort of recess, where a Latin inscription recounts that the Devil, trying to throw him over the precipice, he backed into the cliff, and the cliff opened like wax and (I thinly veil the result in the original Latin) "posteriorem Sancti formam recipit" –

'So farewell beautiful Vallombrosa, farewell "Buena de Lupo" – Wolfs Mouth – from which we looked over Tuscany – Farewell good Dom Basilia – and stupid Fra Benigno and lively, innocent Benedetto –'

They arrived in Rome towards the end of October, and on the 22nd Lady Augusta wrote:

'What will she say when she sees the notice in the Pall Mall about the offensive Article on the Queen's private character published in a Lausanne paper! I see today the Editor has apologised – but how horrid that it shd. be

57

possible – I thought so much of Prss. Hohenlohe today. Pray tell her. I think Rome much more beautiful and cheerful than I expected – As we drove along out came a Dragoon ordering us to alight – then an escort and then Pio Nono in his carriage, talking and laughing with 2 Priests. The people knelt, but there was no enthusiastic reception. I am so glad to have seen him. A most pleasing countenance – A. says he looks upon it as the most venerable temporal Govt. in Europe – in the world – but *temporal*, "par excellence," and the more the famous "tu es Pierre" applies to Peter, the less he feels does it apply to the Pope!! –

Avignon, Nov. 2.

'The world we meet in trains and at table d'hôtes – business people chiefly – seem much discontented. Mexico has shaken their confidence in the Emp: and this new expedition of which they all say "on ne sait pas où cela nous menera" appears to be very unpopular. – One Priest disapproved because he thought in spite of all, that in doing this plain duty there must still be some arrière pensée of imposing terms on the Pope and some understanding with "Le Piémontais" – so that the poor Emperor unless he is very fortunate and clever will please none –The Bp. of Le Puy asked for prayers but especially for money. . . . We went in a bus to Vienne escaping endless delays but O the smoking, spitting and garlic! The beds unclean everywhere – but the eating rooms and the omnibuses to and from stations *reek* – Vienne is a very pretty town with interesting Roman and middle age remains. On our way to Avignon next day we spent two hours at Orange where there is the finest Roman theatre anywhere. – The sunset at Avignon was wonderful.

'. . . An Irish couple travelling with a child and *19 Birds!* amused us much she so alarmed and he so impatient. Another very funny party fraternised with them. The old lady had as many birds and was as fond of them, but then *she* could not bear to expose their nerves to the wear and tear of travelling and so she left hers always "au pension," at the Hotel at Nice.

St. John de Luz, Nov. 5.

'We left Toulouse yesty. and got out at Lourdes, where I saw the castle where our dear Father was imprisoned.[1] A beautiful view but O, what he must have suffered cut off from all there – It made me very sad – '

Gladstone, who was 'extremely enjoying his liberty,' was in Rome, and, with his family, he urged the Dean and Lady Augusta to stay at their hotel, where they 'dined together.' Lady Augusta continued her narrative to her sister.

'The Guardiananno unces Constance's [2] marriage to Ld. Beauchamp today. – The Gladstones give an unsatisfactory report of his temper and crotchets – I hope it is not true.

Nov. 9.

'Mr. Gladstone has no possible understanding of a joke – that, I am sure, is the hitch and the cause of his failing to reap all the benefit he might from his immense talents – Well, yesterday we went to the Catacomb of St. Calixtus. . . . Coming home, it was dark and A. took the youngest Miss Gladstone in his carriage, with Nardi and Rossi while I went with the Americans, the Gladstones having an open one. G. talked of the iniquity of the spoliations of the Italian Govt. etc., and Nardi, turning to

[1] *Her father, Thomas Lord Elgin, was imprisoned at Lourdes by Napoleon.*
[2] Her niece. The marriage did not take place.

Mary G. enquired "Est-ce comme cela chez vous Mlle.? Est-ce que l'on a abrégé le 7ème Commandement? Est-ce qu'il n'existe plus le 7ème Com:? Est-ce qu'on l'a effacé?" – Poor Mary, judge of her feelings?

'At last A. whispered to her "he means the 8th" but she could not even thus reassured command herself to reply to the pressing interrogatories!! (Now you *must* tell me if you like this?) Before knowing this, Mr. G. went on about the beloved N. being unpolished etc., to which I in fury replied that he was more natural than most, which was much more important. He knows nothing of human nature. A Franciscan (learned) was sent to see him and A. today – polished with a vengeance – I think the handsomest man I almost ever saw – such eyes – such a beautiful clear skin – such features – middle age got up within an inch – O such a perfection and so completely aware of it. Speaks equally exquisite French and Italian – sneaky beyond belief I thought – and it turns out he is the official adviser of the French Embassy on ecclesiastical matters!!! "Vous m'en direz tout" – and has liberal views as to the temporal power. . . . Nardi, however, nothing daunted by Gladstone's cool appearance, presented himself to-day and they all met us at St. Peter's at three – he calling the eldest Agnes, or as she fondly imagined "*Signorina* Agnese." '

They went to the Sistine Chapel, 'very beautiful, but the voices are so harsh.' 'Poor [Dean Stanley] had no dress coat and had pinned up the tails of his other. He was ignominiously turned back and had to borrow one at the Hotel, much too large, but the right cut. Gladstone followed and was also turned back. No exceptions could be made.' And to this account by Lady Augusta, the

Dean adds: 'Not all Gladstone's arguments in his best Italian would induce the Guards to concede the point. ... So he remained outside till two cardinals of his acquaintance, passing by, took him in.'

'How anyone can think it impressive and devotional to see the Pope come and go and have have his Mitre taken off and on 20 times, each time clutching his skull cap, I can really not imagine. Those who are used to it may follow (I doubt it) but how those who think there is not enough spirituality and devotion with us, can think there is more there seriously I can not understand. Of course the representations in the Catacombs show that the early Christians prayed standing, but A. has also discovered that the Popes themselves sit and stand, as the Presbyterians do!!!!

'People seem really to think that the Pope has not a leg to stand on – if he persists in refusing to come to terms with the Italians. – His troops are not to be depended on and he himself talks of leaving. –

'I found an extraordinary letter today, purporting to have been received by a Child in a miraculous manner, from Our Lord, published by authority of the Pope – Such things about Indulgences etc., A. is going to take it to Rome and ask Talbot gravely abt. it.'

Dean Stanley had an audience with the Pope while he was in Rome, but the conversation was not as entertaining as on that first occasion, when the Dean was received along with his friend Canon Pearson. Then the Pope resisted

'with dignified courtesy, any attempt to kiss his hand, and pressed us down upon the chairs, where we sate during the colloquy. . . . He spoke of the Queen, and said that she had lately had a great misfortune in being upset out of her carriage in the Highlands.

'I replied, "Yes; but her chief misfortune has been that she has lately lost her excellent husband."

' "Ah, yes!" he said, "that may be, but nevertheless it is a great misfortune to be upset out of your carriage." '

And then had followed the Pope's famous remark about Pusey.

'When you meet him, give him this message from me – that I compare him to a bell, which always sounds to invite the faithful to Church, and itself always remains outside.'

On this second visit, when he was in Rome with Lady Augusta, the Dean went 'in full deaconal costume.' The Pope

'observed and took hold of the cassock which I wore. He said "I have seen something of this kind before. It is the same as an English clergyman once wore in coming to see me. His name was Thompson." '

Thompson turned out to be Townsend,

'who had come in former years on a mission to convert the Pope. The Pope said, with shouts of laughter, "and what do you suppose he came to do? – the most ridiculous thing in the world, to attempt the fusion of the two Churches. What nonsense! . . ."

'When we got up to go away, and I knelt to kiss his hand, he again dwelt on the fact that the cassock was the same which he had seen worn by "Thompson"; and so we parted.'

CHAPTER III

CHAPTER III

1866–7–8.

Lady Augusta returned to the Deanery at Westminster, to find 'The book.' It was the Queen's *Leaves from a Journal in the Highlands,* and she wrote to her sister:

'Helps' apologetic introduction of the author to the public makes my blood boil. There is a perfect chorus of praise in the papers – the Mng. Post says that independently of its being the Queen's Book, it would remain one of the best that ever was written!!!!!

'So *nice* it is – very interesting, making me live all my life over again – but – and one says to oneself – if it had been Ireland she had visited and settled on, instead of Aberdeenshire – the ecstacies and interests that would have grown up would have been just as great – and fenianism would never have existed.'

In December, Lady Augusta was at Windsor, acting as Lady-in-Waiting, and she records the events of Sunday the 11th, when in the evening they

'went to Frogmore . . . sat with Prss. Helena in the beloved Duchess's Library – helped her to write to the D. de Nemours and then had tea – very nice and happy. . . .

65   E

Prss. Louise was most tender and full of sympathy – spoke to me long in the corridor on Friday night.

'On Saturday I was again with H.M. before dinner, most sweet – talked quite as if she had been one of ourselves, asked for the photograph which I sent for and gave her – She was very much struck with it. – Spoke of no affairs of her own. I dined alone with Prss. Louise and the two Boys, both much grown – Sunday A. preached a most striking sermon "When the Son of Man cometh shall He etc., etc.," believing Him to be a question which each can help to answer.

'Prss. Beatrice came to see us, too darling. All asked much about you – most tenderly and looked back to yr. visit with much pleasure. –

Westminster, later.

'I am going with Mrs. Conway [1] at 9. if nothing interferes to visit in the Parish – just to see how things are – Dear Mr. C. and I are very much bent on setting up a lodging house – an old reduced Groom of Bp. Heber's offered himself as a Sunday teacher – but he lives in a thieves' lodging house which made Mr. C. rather hesitate!!!!

'Tell me how your days are divided and arranged – Do you see much of Mdm. de Bunsen [2] – her letters are so *very* striking, quite wonderful. I do not know if her conversation is as much so – but I should think a talk with her would be refreshing – Mat. Arnold came Sunday after Church and talked so pleasantly. – He says that till within the last few Vols. when he seems to have become mad almost, no history is so wonderful in giving the

[1] Wife of Canon Conway, Rector of St. Margaret's.
[2] Widow of Baron de Bunsen, who lived at Carlsruhe.

character of the times of which he treats – as Michelet's History of France – one or two Abrégés of French and European History by him are also invaluable.'

Those who imagine that the Victorians made an orgy of sorrow and bereavement can find much to support their contention, but little in the character and story of Lady Augusta. In almost every year of her life there was the death of some relative or near friend to depress her natural cheerfulness and love of life. In September of 1867 her brother, Sir Frederick Bruce, died in Washington, and she found the courage to suppress her grief and continue her work at Westminster. The following letter from the Queen is printed because it shows how complete was her interest and sympathy with everything that happened in the family life of the Bruces.

Balmoral, September 20th, 1867.

Dearest Augusta,

Words are far too weak to say what I feel on this present dreadful occasion when it has pleased God to take your other most dear brother, in the charm and vigour of his useful and valuable life! 'God's will be done.' 'The Lord hath given and the Lord hath taken away – blessed be the name of the Lord.' To say this is almost impossible, and yet it is all we *can* say! My poor, dear Augusta! *How* much and anxiously have you been in my thoughts after your former anxieties and bereavements – as well as your extreme love and affection for your dear brothers and especially for *him* who has now so suddenly been taken away! Poor dear Fanny's[1] thoughts were constantly with you and her greatest anxiety for you knowing the dreadful

[1] Her sister, Lady Frances Baillie, who was on a visit at Balmoral.

67

blow this wd. be *to you*! It was most distressing for me to have to tell her such dreadful news tho' you know that you both are more like near relations to us than any else, and I felt for and *with* her, with all my heart. It brought back *all* the terrible sorrows of 61 – 62 – 63 to my mind and my heart bled to think of this third terrible blow.

To me and to the Country, this is again an irreparable loss. Oh! How I wished him to remain at home. I will not say more to-day – but you may easily believe how glad we were to have dear Fanny with us, she was so bright and happy – and all to end so fearfully! I long to hear how you are, dearest Guska, and how your other dear sisters and poor dear Mary Elgin will bear this blow! God bless you! You have a kind and gentle Comforter by your side who will deeply grieve for you and share your sorrow! How much that helps one – I know full well.

Ever yours affectionately . . .

V.

Late in the autumn of 1867, the Dean and Lady Augusta left England again, this time for Paris, where they were to stay with their old friend, the famous Madame Mohl, whose friends included people as different as Mrs. Gaskell, who wrote *Cranford*, and Renan, who, when he came to breakfast, had to be entertained secretly. 'I have a niece of sixteen who, if she breakfasts with the arch-heretic, will talk of it in the family . . . so I shall send her out.' Madame Récamier, Tourgenief and Merimée were her friends, and when Browning read Carlyle's letters to her, she thought them 'better than his books.' And one day, when she was dusting her books 'in an apron' and an 'old blue silk gown, now on its last legs, with a few rents in it . . . Julie banged open the door and announced the Queen of Holland.'

Madame Mohl was a striking little personality; very old-fashioned in her appearance, with a shock of curly hair surrounding a little face which sparkled with vivacity and humour. She spoke rapidly and wittily and had an extraordinary power of making every society that was round her alive. Society flocked to her famous salons, which went on for many years in Paris, attracting all the most interesting people of the time.

The Dean and Lady Augusta had first met at Madame Mohl's house in the Rue du Bac and she was 'very proud of having had a hand in forming such a prosperous union.' She wrote about the time of the wedding, saying that she had invited a few of 'our mutual friends for the purpose' of toasting her.

'Two days ago I heard it was to be on the 16th, and I altered the day to it; now I am told Lord Elgin is dead, but I can't help it, and shall make no more alterations; so the people will come, and we shall drink some champagne to her, married or not. It seems Arthur is as much in love as if he were twenty or rather, perhaps, as if he were a good deal older than he is; old passions are stronger than young ones.'

Madame Mohl had visited Lady Augusta at the Deanery at Westminster in 1864. One afternoon, Lady Augusta went to her in her bedroom and said, 'Put on your cap and come and see the Queen.' Her Majesty had called and when Madame Mohl was presented, she went down on one knee 'very prettily,' and kissed the Queen's hand.

'My dear, I felt quite emotioned,' she said afterwards. She had asked the Queen about war and the Queen had said, 'No; we shall have no war.' She wrote later:

'I believe that the real reason why we have not had war is that the Queen would not. But her influence is so occult that no one ever alludes to it without saying "So people say on the Continent." I asked Lady Augusta, who knows more than anyone, straight out.

'She answered, "Oh, certainly; her wishes have had some influence." But Lady Augusta says what she pleases, and not what she knows.'

That was in 1864. Three years passed before the Dean and Lady Augusta returned the visit, during which Lady Augusta was dejected and quiet, after the death of her brother, Sir Frederick Bruce. Madame Mohl wrote a slight record of the visit to her niece.

'On the 16th [of October] Lady Augusta and her husband came, and you may think how busy I was during the week they spent here, all the more that the Queen of Holland, who came to see me in September, before my visit to Stors, asked me to arrange an evening for her. I was obliged to look up the few people now here whom I thought she would find agreeable – M. Thiers at the head of them.

'. . . Lady Augusta wished to stay upstairs on account of her brother's death; but the Queen declared she would go up to see her, so Augusta came down and remained with us. Arthur said he was very glad to bring her here to distract her thoughts from the extreme sadness of this death.'

Dean Stanley left a record of his meeting with Thiers, when

'the conversation turned almost entirely upon the alleged discovery by M. Charles of the correspondence between Pascal and Newton asserting that the theory of gravitation was due to the French, and not to the English philosopher. Thiers was entirely persuaded of the truth of this fiction. He was at this time devoted to astronomy, and he took up this theory with the greatest admiration.'

Lady Augusta and the Dean went from Paris to Vienne, Orange, and Avignon. At Avignon, they went to see John Stuart Mill. They

'found him alone, reading . . . first going to the cemetery, to see his wife's tomb . . . beautifully kept in order.'

From Toulouse, on November 2nd, Lady Augusta wrote to Madame Mohl:

'We travelled yesty. with a most delightful gentleman whom we discovered to be a Ct. de Durkheim or Turk-heim, an Alsatian, with German learning and French vivacity combined, and who suddenly astonished the respectable inmates of the 1st class, by exclaiming at Bezies, "Ah, and how near France was to become Pro-testant then, and who can put a limit to the good that would have ensued. She would have grown and strength-ened and then . . . she would not have had that bon vieux Père de Rome to be constantly putting on his legs again and des petites soeurs comme l'Espagne, la Mexique, etc., etc., to be looking after!!!" It was like an electric shock among them! Certainly the Vieux Pères of preced-ing generations have a good deal to answer for in these

71

regions. People seem little satisfied with the present state of things.'

They returned to London in the middle of November. They resumed their work at the Deanery and, on New Year's Day, 1868, Lady Augusta wrote to her sister:

'A. gave such a *beautiful* little extempore sermon at the Hospital after *evensong*! at 6. – I told him it might have been N. MacLeod. – I told you of his Palestine Sermon at 4 p.m. on Saturday at St. Lawrence Jewry – and his indignation at having to wear under his surplice a cassock with tiny buttons from top to toe like the Romans. He could not recover these useless buttons – can you see him struggling with them!!!'

January 26.

'I was going to lend you my "Journal" [the Queen's book] but since the Duke has done so I need not. – I wonder what he thinks of it and Pss. Hohenlohe? The only thing I think in reading it over is that the innocence is so great, the things about the Children and their lessons are so attractive that they disarm – and one may (the public) imagine that the weighty, important thoughts and observations, which no doubt exist, may be left out on purpose, only the insignificant details being safe to publish! The conscientious and faithful record of the Luncheons shew, to us at least, that the text has not been tampered with – and tho' we have a very painful feeling abt. the domestic notes and histories, they give people the idea of a patriarchal system, quite alien from their conception of Royal habits, – and convince them that all are on the same footing. Sir J. Elphinstone expressed his rejoicing over the book and his anxiety that it should be

72

published in a cheap form – the sooner the better. He thought it *most important*. I said I feared the comments of the more educated classes, but he assured me he had not heard a word even in the Clubs. Arthur thinks it a very curious turn of the wheel of fortune that the reception should have been what it is – more favourable than the life [of the Prince Consort]. – I believe the affair of the proposal in the latter and the undignified sort of passages in the matrimonial relation that ruffled so many in the first, and this, since the wrath of the world on the various subjects appears to have blown itself off, and during the lull, the "fond" of true love for Her, has inclined people to put the very best interpretation on the whole – God grant that She may take the kind welcome in the spirit Mr. Martin describes – It is for Her I most lament all this flattery – and this encouragement, when it is least wanted. Reviewers are so totally ignorant. For instance, outside people believe that Royalty lives in the clouds, quite apart from common mortals and that they are served by invisible hands. The idea that its great danger is from being thrown on uneducated people, as none of us are, has never entered their minds, and the delight at the discovery that they treat their servants like human beings is the one point in the Book of which they lay hold. Reeve in the Edin[burgh] *Review* has a most stupid bombastic passage, Samuel, of Oxford, a worse in the *Quarterly*, with this judicious addition that it is only with *Scottish Servants* one could be on such blessed terms!!!! These ignorant, stupid remarks are calculated to do great harm to our dear One – but I can only hope that these minor things may be swept away in the flood of thankfulness Mr. M. describes – Beloved Ly. Car[oline Barrington] came to tea on Wedy.

Blessed Car is much less hostile to the Book than I expected, but she quoted some man as having said "it is pretty but a great mistake." '

Jany. 30/68.

My own darling,

How sad you will be to hear of dear P. Leopold['s illness] – Prss Louise's letter came last night, Mr. Duckworth's[1] this morning – both are most affecting – He had been unusually well and in Dec. he looked quite strong and healthy, a wholesome colour and manly bearing and had improved in every way – I can not but hope, having seen him rally so often and from such severe attacks when all hope seemed gone. Darling Boy – God's will be done – if He is taken, I feel it will be from a life of great trial. But I trust he may be spared for good. There is something so natural and true in Pss Louise's letter – so the reverse of the wordiness characteristic of most of this young generation. The Bp. of London and A. have been bothered to death by this threatened clandestine consecration of a new Natal Bishop[2] – The fanatics who are pushing it on

---

[1] His tutor.

[2] Following the affair of Bishop Colenso, who had been excommunicated by the Archbishop of Cape Town, for expressions of heresy in a book of which he was the author. When the case of Bishop Colenso came before the English Church authorities some years before, Dean Stanley was ardent in his support of the Bishop and later expressed his faith in Colenso by inviting him to preach at Westminster. The Queen approved of the Dean's championship of Doctor Colenso and in later letters She asked the Dean to convey her private approval of the Natal Bishop's 'noble, disinterested conduct in favour of the natives who were so unjustly used.' In a letter to Lord Carnavon on the matter, She wished 'the natives and coloured races should be treated with every kindness and affection' and She wishes that '*all* her colonial Governors should *know* her feelings on this *subject* of the *native races*.'

aim, it is thought, at the severance of Church and State by setting the Law at defiance – The poor Archbishop is so weak – says *yes* to everyone – The Bp. of Oxford plays fast and loose – It is too sad to see the good Bp. of London's precious strength exhausted by such inutilities.

. . . Did I tell you that I took Longfellow down to Windsor, a delightful tête à tête, there and back. He is so charming. She [the Queen] was much pleased with him and he had a few words with Pr. Leo and Prss. Louise besides. . . .

Lady Augusta did not narrow the society at the Deanery down to either the Dean's ecclesiastical associates or her own friends. The Dean's politics were Liberal and this fact brought Gladstone and his associates within his circle. Yet the Tories came, the scientists, the poets and the musicians. Lady Augusta achieved a tremendous good in entertaining members of the Royal Family and the brilliant commoners of the day at the same time. She took Longfellow to the Queen, and invited the Princes and Princesses to dinner at the Deanery to meet Tennyson, Browning and Carlyle, and scientists, such as Tyndall and Owen. After such a dinner the Princess Royal wrote to her:

Dearest Augusta and dear Dean,
    I did *so* enjoy the dinner and the party – so kindly and so beautifully arranged. – I *wish* I could have stayed longer for how can one feel tired in such charming society. I hope my leaving so soon did not appear rude and that no one is angry with me for doing so. – I had a trying day – and have a deal before me tomorrow. Pray make Jenny Lind write into my book also. How am I to thank my

kind and amiable hosts for the pleasant hours just passed.
My only regret is that my Husband should have been
away – there are so many people he would have liked to
have seen and I am sure there were many who would
have been glad to see him.

Goodbye and goodnight.

> Yrs. sincerely and affectly. and gratefully,
> VICTORIA.

Early in 1868, Lady Augusta joined the Court at
Osborne, where she found

'everything was most pleasant and most cheery. . . . The
Queen and they all dwelt on P. Alfred's escape – on the
wickedness a little – but not as much as I expected and
mercifully, it did not seem to take hold of their imagina-
tions or make them nervous, which is a great blessing –
H.M. said "people write now more than when Leo was
so ill and yet this, when I know Affie safe, is nothing to
me like the agony of watching that struggle between life
and death for so many days" –

'The Abyssinian news was very doubly welcome coming
as it did. It is a most happy and most glorious thing. –
Pss. Helena is quite mad about politics – *for* Dizzy and
against Gladstone. . . . A. is unhappy because he thinks
that the friends of the I. Church are as dangerous as
the Enemies – the "no surrender" as wrong as the clap
trap of Gladstone whose sudden conversion to the opportunity of the move, made him stop the whole business
of the country to bring forward a move he cannot
explain, and the carrying out of which he has not dreamt
of considering – But Pss. Helena is wild about Dizzy (I

think he must have spread his butter very thick). The Queen is much pleased with him but not so engouée. Pss. Louise sees her sister's onesidedness and is rather severe upon it. Pr. Christian is very wise and grave and tolerant and just, but does not modify or control his wife's opinions apparently much. . . . Mrs. W. Grey I saw much at Osborne. She is a *jewel* and a rare friend for them. She was much struck with the Queen's kindness and only anxious to make the young ones respond properly to it. She tells me since that the Pss. of Wales was profoundly impressed by the Irish welcome and the beauty of the country and the charm of the people! Mrs. G. says she is much matured and appreciates things as she did not in her early days. I dined with H.M. on the 12th and went to the St. Thomas foundation stone next morning. She looked too pretty and touching. I could not keep from weeping when I saw Her. She was very amiable the evg. before – wanted me to go down today till Sunday – but I have the house full, Liddels, Thomsons etc., and asked to return tomorrow.'

Deanery, March 23.

'. . . You know what a scurry I had – the telegram ordering me to Windsor for the night and the note offering the [Prince and Princess] Christians to dine on Tuesday reached me after church on Sunday – imagine the scrimmage. . . . By dint of telegrams we collected a charming party of literati and old friends of the family – darling Harriet [1] – such a delight to see her and have her – the blessed one – dear Car. Parnell and Carlyle who sat by the Pss. (and talked even on Froude) Browning, Kinglake,

[1] The Hon. Mrs. Preston Bruce, daughter of Lord Rivers, a great beauty who had been Maid of Honour to the Queen at her coronation.

Tyndall, A. Russell. . . . In the evening M. Arnold, our own Chapter magnates and a few who could not see them otherwise. H. was very happy and dear, quite amiable and civil and recalling to Harriet so exactly her mother's manner – He [Prince Christian] . . . really enjoyed it and would have liked a few additional hours to deliver himself of all he had to say!! Told me he used to love acting –

' "Tragedies," I suggested.

' "No, comedies, farces!!"

'Cha.[1] was a host in herself. . . . You may imagine how my head ached after such an affair, but it was all quite successful.'

She wrote to Madame Mohl, in April:

'. . . Arthur has been working very hard – the second edition of "The Memorials," many sermons and a whole host of little darts, with sheets of writing against the religious and political evils and iniquities that are going on. I fear he stands more and more alone, for he generally finds his friends as little to be agreed with and as much requiring to be testified against as his enemies. But every now and then I hear of those outside the mass who look on – and who are cheered and helped and consoled by the stand he makes. I am very glad indeed that you and M. Mohl go to the de Broglies, both for the sake of Mm. de Stael and for the sake of the old Duke – besides I think it very good for the Prince to come in contact with wise people.'

[1] Her sister, Lady Charlotte Locker.

CHAPTER IV

Lady Augusta and the Dean in Ireland. Lady Augusta's letters to her sister and to the Queen.

CHAPTER IV

In August, 1868, they went to Ireland, and the story of
their holiday is told in a series of long letters written by
Lady Augusta, opening 'in Dublin bay,' where they
arrived 'at 7':

It was a fine night and the Boats certainly are splendid.
We came to this charming Hotel, were raised to the 3rd –
in a lift, had breakfast and sallied forth to Church. But O
the Cars!! What they are? When we reached Sackville
St. I entreated to be let down. I was quite moist with
terror. It seemed to me impossible to find any position
in which you can be safe from being shot across the street
at any moment, hold on as you might. And the bumping!
Our horse was ready to jump or start or bolt or anything
besides. We went to enquire at the Metropolitan Chapel
for Father Burke. All the authorities were consulted, but
in vain. He was advertised to preach there, and at another place out of town (to which they advised us to go
in a 'bus) at the same moment. But even they saw the
difficulty of his accomplishing this, and the advice they
gave us was of so uncertain and contradictory a character,
we abandoned the attempt. A Te Deum was to be sung
for the recovery of the Cardinal – but whether from
inflammation of the *brain* or *bowels* (for he had heard both

81   F

mentioned) our informant could not say. 'We poor Catholics, we have the impression that God hears our prayers and so, you see, we ask everything. Ah, but this time it's thanksgiving.'

Whether he had the same impression about that, we could not make out!

We went then to Ch. Ch. Cathedral and having been shown into a seat, a strange looking gent came up and said he was in a delicate position there, being the son of a late Dean, but he felt sure the present would wish Arthur to occupy *his* pew and tho' Lady Augusta has a seat *in her own right* as a *Peeress*, I daresay she would still like to go with you (to A.)! We accepted – and I received my right. – The music was good, but the Sermon Hibernian. On coming out Arthur's impression of the whole concern was that the Country is too *ridiculous* to make anything of anyway. – He went to St. Patrick's in the afternoon – and then we drove round the Phoenix Park, calling to ask what had happened abt. Father Burke on the way. He had not been seen or heard of!

The Park is too beautiful. I even forgot my car to admire it and at last found my balance and could look forward with calm to the future. The beautiful trees and the background of the Wicklow mountains, quite exquisite. I thought so much of dear Robert [General Bruce who was Governor to the Prince of Wales] he loved it so much in the old days. –

Clifden (Connemara). Sep. 3.

We were driven from Limerick by the Shannon by the Bishop and Mrs. Graves. We had Luncheon with a Capt. and Mrs. Vansittart at Castle Connell, rowed down the River and walked back along its banks. It bends most picturesquely there and is beautifully wooded so that, tho' the latter are flat, it is a very pretty scene. After a cup of tea we parted with the kind Graves couple, and our Hosts sent us on to Killaloe, where the Brother Bishop received us. The Palace is an ordinary looking country house – in a wooded Park, with glimpses of the river. He is the enchanting Bp. who wrote to A. about the vestment question, as illustrated by a Canon of the early Irish Church, forbidding Presbyters to go naked!!! – He is quite charming, really broken hearted for the loss of his wife 8 years ago. But with such a sense of humour that these things come out in spite of himself. Besides this, he is, Arthur thinks, one of the most distinguished minds among the Bps. whether Irish or English, and an admirable man. He is of course very unhappy. If things are overthrown it will only be another example of the lesson that the children do suffer for the faults of the Fathers and reap what they have sown, for never in the History of the Ch: was there a time of such promise, or anything like the movement towards better things than has been within the last 10 or 15 years.

The Bp. of Killaloe has one grown-up and two little daughters and three sons at College – all good and clever, but so shy and awkward. It is quite curious. There was a very charming Clergyman the first day at dinner who gave us a description of his position in his Parish that made one's mouth water. – Such a good and happy influence. –

Tuesday we drove to a place on the Shannon, which above K. expands into a Lake (Lough Derg) and after Luncheon we were taken in a boat to Holy Island, a lovely sail and back – Our poor hosts had lost their two only children just growing up – and O so good they are – taking to life again and burying their own anguish in the effort to do good to all specially to young people!!! – We had lovely weather and were delighted – Yesty. morning at 8 the Bp. sent us to Nenagh 10 miles off, whence we posted in cars 45 miles (no joke) halting at Clonmacnoise to visit the ruins of a famous collection of 7 Churches. A beautiful situation overlooking an immense plain, golden brown in the setting sunlight (from the grass on the moor) and bounded by a range of light blue hills in the shadowy distance. A vulgarish party of young people, with a Priest were there. The moment they saw us, they began declaiming against the English at the top of their voices (the lay ones), the climax of their wrath being reserved for an inscription in the old wall, recording what had been done in the way of restoration by the Soc: of Antiquaries.

How they dared to put their names there – how the Irish people could submit etc., etc. –

A. and I separated and, each addressing our nearest neighbour, asked if they knew Rome, for that was just what could be seen on all the old monuments, only the slabs were much larger and more disfiguring, which recorded the names and deeds of the Popes! –

My man became suddenly more subdued. A.'s, who was the Priest, writhed a good deal, but could only hasten to get away.

An old woman, a guide, told us the most excellent stories of miracles performed at the old consecrated spots and shewed where King —— had driven away St. Finian's cow – how the Saint had announced that in consequence, he would die of thirst, and how truly enough the Shannon dried up and he did die, the Shannon flowing again when he was disposed of! – Wonderful tales – at St. F.'s Well there is a thorn bush covered with little rags and bits of thread and string, left there by Pilgrims, to prove they had performed the pilgrimage and that the Saint may not forget them.

Leenone, Saturday.

There is a curious quarter of the town at Galway built of small detached cottages, thatched, called the Claddagh and inhabited by the fishermen and women who form a separate community of Newhaven. The people generally are supposed to have much Spanish blood. They are dark and handsome and the women, with their red petticoats and white, or red or blue cloaks, walking as erect as possible, look most picturesque. Some of the old houses are built like Spanish ones, with a sort of court. We started at 11., on one car, luggage and all, and had a lovely drive to Oughterard, 14 miles. There the market was going on and, since Freyburg in Germany, I never saw so pretty a sight – the red handks. over their white caps, the cloaks and petticoats, the men with breeches, long stockings and impossible coats. It was a lovely day and the village itself very picturesque. There was also the yearly fair of Cattle at Galway and we met crowds of peasants from the Highlands of Connemara, bringing their ponies and beasts for sale. We had two horrid horses and cars to take us on to Clifden, where we arrived late. It is the headquarters of the Irish Church Mission and there are new District Churches and Schools springing up in these wilds. Mr. D'Arcy, the Rector, was a large landed proprietor. He did much for the people during the famine and had to sell his estate (which is now in the hands of a fool English Cath:) but he was so much beloved and respected that he has continued to have great influence and has carried on his mission work with much success. They have a charming female orphanage, presided over by a Lady who has been the mother of these children for 17 years, and another for boys, also admirably conducted. Their controversy rather takes one's breath away. It is like Anna's turned inside out – but tho' it rather startles one – I do not know that there is any other way of dealing with Irish people, and surely it must be good to cultivate the Protestant element – if it were only for the W.C.'s it brings with it –

A farmer was told he ought really to erect one in his garden. 'Sure and that I can't' says he – 'they would take me for a convert'!!

Mr. D'Arcy was ill and we could not see him, but we saw his Wife and Curates and the people of the school, and O, such healthy, rosy, clean, nice children they are, and all taken out of the filthy pig stye cabins.

Clifden is in a far inland Bay. On leaving it we went by the Coast – beautiful and studded with islands and promontories. On leaving we found Lake upon Lake and finally, a sort of Fiord, on the banks of which at Leenone, we halted for the night, in a most primitive hotel. On our road to Clifden we drove for miles and miles thro' the district that belonged to Col. Martin, the sort of King of Connemara, but whose property has now passed from the family.

Leenone.

Arthur's face on Friday evening, dining in the Coffee room with two English *Gents* and a Lady who talked sport at the top of their voices all the time *to* and *at* him, was quite 'impayable.' There was nothing but the fattest of

86

mutton and a goose to be had and the horrid people in the Private sitting room got the goose! Yesty. morning (Sunday Ly. L. Castle MacGarrett) we made an expedition of three hours on the Lake from Leenone and then came on to Westport in a car – *roasting hot,* drove about Lord Sligo's place and the Bay – and came on here at 8 by train –

Our fellow passenger was an Irish Skipper who had been making a '*tower* of pleasure' since Monday, and had been so happy he did not think he had been asleep above 10 minutes at a time, night or day. It was not that *scenerys* were new to him, he had been all over the world and the handsomest scenery he had seen was at Venice – not a horse or a *car* in the streets. You can only go about in Gon*dollos*. He challenged us to imagine the amazement of his wife when she saw him walk in, as this morning, for each place he had stopped at he had written – 'I am here, will write by next post' – how could she from that guess he was on his way home? – Arthur's face was good then also!!

Lord Oranmore is charming, so intelligent and amiable. She is Scottish, good, but rather cold – the place comfortable and Protestant in essentials!! but not very pretty – we go to Tuam tomorrow, then to Armagh, where we shall be till the 12th.

Ld. Oranmore says that the negative effect of the Establisht. is so very important and he mentioned what we had noticed, the astonishing absence of glaringly idolatrous practices here, as compared with abroad – The presence of the enlightened minority and in most Parishes, of an educated man, is a most powerful check to much that would else be rampant, for the Priests, having the power they have, the standard of education

87

and spiritual teaching would at once drop, were these restraints to be removed.

Here the servants come to Prayers – Ld. O. never asks the Priest and nothing is said, whereas good kind excellent Miss FitzGerald is only allowed to read a Chapter to her 'Bess,' and the party is then commanded by the Priest to quit, before the Prayers!! Lord O. says you must even them to allowing or not allowing – He is a great Liberal, treats them like fellow Christians. But he has the greatest horror of the *system*, from seeing it at work and just talks like you Cha. abt. Nuns and Priests!

Sept. 7.

There is a delicious dancing master in the village here – quite a character. He never employs words of less than four syllables and evidently teaches 'maintien,' like Bobby's friend. The late Lord Dunkellin, who had been his pupil, met him in later life, when he had taken to stooping. Lord D. asked him if he could do anything for him – and was answered in a tragic tone, 'Yes, *never* say who was yr. dancing master.'

I asked if he would not be sent for today for the Children, but heard that at this season, he is engaged in getting in his potatoes!

Palace, Armagh, September 11th.

Bishop Bernard and his good wife received us most lovingly. He is Lord Bandon's brother, a most excellent man and rector for twenty four years of his father's parish, where he and his wife were adored. . . . So good, but with plenty of Irish wit and readiness. The Palace is a square house in a small park opening into the town. . . . They have a pretty flower garden and that and their park they open to the people of all classes, and put seats for them. Never a leaf is touched. . . . The Dean is a tremendous controversialist and at one time could not stir without two policemen, such was the rage of the Romans against him. But he has lived it down and is now respected. . . . The thing he said was that he could not bear the word *serious* – why came good people to be debarred from fun? . . . The young Bernard ladies were here and to our amazement we discovered that they call their very reverend Uncle and his wife 'Jane and Charlie.' Such a respected, venerable Charlie. . . . We met with many interesting people there. . . . One of the Abyssinian captives, Kearns. He went out at seventeen with Captain Speed to hunt etc., when Captain Speed left he was taken by Cameron as secretary, was sent up with despatches, those in which the Queen's expected letter was not, and taken with Cameron and the others. The account of those four and a half years was terrible, the misery, the filth, the insults, and the horrible scenes they had to witness – burning of whole families, mutilation and execution of numbers of captives – the cutting off of the hands and feet of victims, so as to save time in taking off the fetters which could not be wasted!!

Oct. 2.

I left off at Garron Tower, that wonderful place on the Antrim Coast, which charmed our eyes, even when they had just feasted on the '*handsome little Bays*' of the Giant's Causeway. On a clear day you see all the Coast of Scotland and all the Coast of Ireland. If I could tell you what those 26 miles of road are, out right round the cliffs, through every sort of obstacle. The morning was lovely and the red cliffs and white cliffs and black cliffs – and the green foliage of the limestone vegetation in places – all contrasting with the blue water, was exquisite. After hurrying us off at 7, not in a tandem car alas! but in a phaeton of the most lumbering sort, we reached Larne, the station (and place where Ed: Bruce landed) an hour before the starting of the train. This hour A. devoted to bathing and I found him, the day being boiling hot, setting out with his immense red rug cuddled up in his arms, to walk a mile. I asked for what purpose.

'O, I have no towel, I am taking this instead'!!!!

I persuaded him to trust to what we might find and a nice woman in a cottage lent us one, for which she was quite unwilling to receive payment, and a man seeing us with it, flew to offer advice as to a bathing place – so obliging they are.

Imagine my feelings on seeing a sloop at the quay from St. Andrew's, Fife! I could not find the Skipper alas! –

A curious feature of the Larne station was the outburst of Protestant feeling, on the walls of a certain abode, which, to be sure, might have been doubly dear to travellers of that persuasion, coming from Donegal!! – 'To H. with the Pope. K. William for ever, etc., etc., etc., etc.!!!'

Some Lady of a different way of thinking had written a strong appeal – 'Such *indecent* writing should indeed be avoided *especially* by females' – and she went on to say that she felt inclined to think that it would even be the duty of the railway authorities to interpose to prevent it – but to me it seems *rather* difficult to understand how this can be done. – Shd. each Lady be accompanied by a Porter, whose duty it would be to watch, or how? –

The rail to Belfast is also by the coast, along the shore, and Belfast Lough among trees and gardens and cultivated fields – the Lough itself blue and shining, being studded with white sails.

You pass Carrickfergus, where E. Bruce held his court and where William landed, and reach Belfast.

We took a train which led us along the opposite side of the Lough, to Clandeboy station where Ld. Dufferin's carriage met us. The road is as lovely as the opposite one, a long avenue thro' Ld. D.'s grounds leads to his house. There a grand rifle match was going on, but we made him leave it to drive us to a Tower, built in honour of his Mother from the top of which you see the whole world on a clear day. At dinner we met several of the Belfast Professors – and the head of the Wesleyan College – a Mr. Arthur who was the coadjutor of dear —. He is good, but narrow, and one could only wonder that a body rich enough to build the splendid College we had seen, could not produce a more distinguished chief.

Belfast is most flourishing, more like Glasgow, but not nearly so dirty. Lady Dufferin is delicate but very gentle and pleasing. He, very agreeable – He has in his house most interesting relics, brought home by him from the East and all arranged with taste. – He speaks much of the flourishing condition of Ireland in reality and its wonderful progress during the last years (which must indeed be, if the old accounts are true) in contradistinction to the gloomy pictures drawn by politicians. He however is, I believe, with Gladstone, more or less, about the Church, though he contends that in other matters all would be well if they were only left alone. In a general way the

Church people say the Land question is the grievance the people really feel. The enemies of the Church made light of the land – so does Moriarty, the R. Bp. of Kerry for instance.

Next morning at 8. we were off again by rail to Belfast – walked from one station to another – passed in the train thro' Lisburn, a flourishing manufacturing place, founded by banished Huguenots – where Jeremy Taylor is buried, to Newry where the Claremont's carriage met us and carried us to Ravensdale, their lovely place, where we lunched and walked about. Ld. and Ly. C. are most dear and charming people. We wished we could have remained, but we had to move on and they sent us to Dundalk, 7 miles, a very pretty road by the sea, and the Carlingford Mountain and the Hill, on which Ed. Bruce is buried.

While waiting for the car to take us on – we went into the Inn and issuing forth, were seized by half a doz. harpies who demanded alms and nearly tore our things off. It was the worst specimen of begging we had met with.

A long dreary drive brought us to Lough Fea, the abode of Mr. E. Shirley of Warwickshire. Their great estates are in England but by marriage they inherited half of the Irish estates bestowed by Elizabeth on Essex. No one had thought of living there until his Father took a fancy to the country and created an oasis in the midst of the surrounding desert, by the side of a pretty Lake. You need only plant in Ireland – everything grows and in no time you have splendid woods. The house is beautiful and contains a library of 2,000 volumes, all on Ireland! He is a charming man – she delightful.

A HOLIDAY IN IRELAND

We found among the guests Mr. Holmes of the B. Museum who had been with the Abyssinian Expedition – After dinner we were shewn into a splendid Baronial Hall, where about thirty neighbours came to spend the evening. – One most dear elderly, fat lady, coiffé en cheveux, with pink flowers, proved to be the widow of a Brother of Mr. Russell's, who was a 'mauvais sujet.' Such a dear she was – Next day we unwillingly bid adieu to these nice people and went on to the Bp. of Meath's.

Next day A. shewed such unmistakable signs of being determined to see the ruins of *Trim* that the poor Bp. took us, the rain and storm coming on in a fearful way. The ruins are very fine – a Castle and two Abbeys of the Norman time, on the banks of the Boyne. The Rector was charming and hospitable and his sister supplied me with dry clothes, after our archeological expedition! In the evening we had, as at Lough Fea, an evening party. Mrs. Butcher, the Bp.'s wife, is a most warm-hearted, kind, pleasing person, with eyes that go thro' you. The Dean of Cork and his wife were there, and a Being you would love beyond expression. The Chief Justice Whiteside. He never pauses and his conversation is one continuous flow of wit. At breakfast we sat on and on – the Butler making periodical inroads, like Shirley and finally, his patience being exhausted, he brought his suite and commenced carrying off the dishes. He, Whiteside, sang the Grove of Blarney for us, with many apologies on behalf of his position and station.

Saturday, we made the poor Bp. take us to the Hill of Tara and 'Tara's Halls,' and there we parted, he for home and we in a car, thro' Beaupre and Slane, by the Boyne – the two houses are perched on the high-wooded banks, at

93

the most picturesque angles of the river, which winds beautifully – The rain came on in torrents, but A. was very anxious, notwithstanding that and the darkness, to take a circuitous mountain road in order to see something [a prehistoric monument]. This I mercifully overruled. As it was we only got to the station by dark – *drenched* – and then had tea, while waiting for the train for Malahide. – A very rough looking Priest was sitting with a friend by the refresht. room fire – they were *not* drinking *tea* by any means. We had been shocked at Drogheda, when we passed there before, by the sight of a placard abt. a lottery for the Xtian Brothers Schools – He, the Priest, told us with pride how a young girl had won the £50 prize and we modestly asked if that did not encourage gambling. He scorned the idea, tho' some persons held it and quoted the parliamentary candidate, a Mr. Whitworth, a teetotaller and an Independent, as encouraging the lottery – but that, he owned, might be to make political capital out of it! –

We reached Malahide at 10 – and dressed for the party in the House. Lord T[albot] is a great archeologist and a very nice man. – Ly. T. is I believe excellent – a great friend of Mrs. Boyle – She looks much older than Ld. T. and altogether as if she does not belong to the affair – but that is nonsense. The family have resided there since the Norman Conquest and the Castle is the oldest inhabited house in Ireland, very quaint and handsome, with interesting pictures. But O, the smells of cooking, petroleum, oil, etc., etc., etc. I could not rest with such smells.

Malahide town or village is much more civilized looking than I expected and the view from the rising ground, over Dublin and Malahide Bay – quite lovely. On Monday we returned to Drogheda by an early train and took a car with which to revisit the Boyne battle field, the curious prehistoric monument which A. had so unwillingly missed on Saturday and which I *really* congratulated myself on having quenched, on the dark, wet night, when I found that you have to enter on *hands and knees*!!

The day was beautiful. We found ourselves on the spot where K. William stood, just at 10 a.m., in bright sunlight – the very hour at which the English army crossed the river. You understand the whole scene, with Macaulay in hand – The sepulchral monument, A. said, migh have been built by the same people who built the pyramids. It is the same sort of idea and construction 'en petit.'

From there we drove to Slane Abbey, a ruin in a commanding position. Then to Mellifont, the first Cistercian Abbey, founded by St. Malachi, a friend of St. Bernard's, and on to the ruins of Monasterboice, where are the finest crosses in Ireland. We caught the train again at Drogheda and got back to Malahide, to sleep and dine. Next morning, we went to Dublin by 9. Here A. heard the Dean of Cork's sermon and we saw and heard all we could during the day – dined, had a party and slept at the Provost's (Trinity College) and left at 5.30 a.m. The crossing was rough – but I escaped by lying down in a nice deck cabin. At Holyhead Mr. and Mrs. W. Stanley met us with flowers and grapes and we had most exquisite weather and views all the way, arriving here at 7 p.m. –

Lady Augusta wrote a long letter to the Queen during the Irish tour, and from the 'Donegal Highlands' she wrote:

'The people, who are strong and handsome, are of a less mixed race than in many other parts, more purely

Celtic. We dined and slept at a most primitive House of "entertainment," where one of Your Majesty's Highland inn chickens would have been a delicacy indeed. *Even* the Dean could not swallow what they offered to us! But that was nothing to him, as he was tracking St. Columba's footsteps. . . . How much I hope that Your Majesty may some day be able to see some of the peculiar beauties of Irish scenery, as Your Majesty says, and I am certain that Your Majesty in no degree over-estimates the good that would result from it. The people are very sensitive and so alive to anything that honours them and their country and *raises them and it* in their own estimation and in the scale of nations. . . . A lady who lives near Powers Court told me that she had been much struck by the observations of her Scotch gardener, a most keen and intelligent man, at the time and after the visit of the Prince and Princess of Wales. . . . Many whom he knew well to be filled with the most hostile theories, gradually warmed and warmed, when the theoretical *abstractions* which they thought of at a distance with such bitter feelings, were brought face to face with them in the form of *Persons* whom they could look on and honour, and who were ready to welcome and appreciate them and their Country. – If they could find some day that the Highlands of Donegal or of Connemara or their wild iron bound coasts, which so few visit, were admired and appreciated by Your Majesty, and that the poetic legends and traditions of their land and language kindle in Your Majesty the interest I know they would, – it would warm and cheer and fill with enthusiasm, thousands and thousands of hearts. – Your Majesty's experience of Gaelic would make it easier to understand and retain the names than we found it.'

CHAPTER V

The Prince and Princess of Wales' visit to Denmark:
Colonel Keppel's letters. The Princess and a lobster. Paris criticism of the Queen. Her relations
with the Empress. The King of Sweden. The
Prince of Wales made a Freemason.

G

1868.

Both the Dean and Lady Augusta were untiring letter-writers. Indeed, it was said that long and late hours of writing was one of the causes of her illness and death. Thus, while they made Westminster a centre of spiritual good, intellectual stimulus and social interest, they corresponded with a diverse and scattered company of friends: Madame Mohl, in Paris, the Queen of Holland, the English Princesses who had gone to live in Germany, friends in Canada and America, and nearer, their associates in Oxford. And when their English friends went abroad, they usually chose Lady Augusta or the Dean for a series of long letters. And such letters, preserved with Lady Augusta's papers, give pictures of many events of the time. Among their mutual friends was Lieut.-Colonel F. Keppel, who had accompanied the Prince of Wales, the Dean, and General Bruce, on their tour of the East in 1862. He wrote constantly to them in the years which followed, and two of his letters of 1868, when he accompanied the Prince and Princess of Wales to Denmark, give an interesting picture which may be recorded here.

My dear Moth (he wrote to Dean Stanley, from Fredensborg Castle, on December 1st):

You must excuse my beginning this irreverently, but I feel if I commence with 'dear Mr. Dean,' I shall have in my mind a pedagogue in an M.A. gown (why M.A. I can't say) and armed with a birch rod, so you would receive but a stiff formal letter, which I do not wish to be the case with my old travelling companion of 62.

I duly conveyed your thanks for the game to H.R.H. I will now write as you request a *private confidential* but accurate and truthful account of our proceedings.

We (i.e. Their R.H. and three eldest children, L[ad]y Carmarthen, Sir W. Knollys, etc.) left London on the 17th ult. by the night mail from Charing Cross Station, where . . . a considerable crowd had assembled, who cheered Their R.H. loudly on their departure, and similar demonstrations took place on their embarkation at Dover. The passage across the Channel was a rapid one, but a considerable delay occurred at Calais, owing to the necessity of weighing our baggage which consisted of over 250 (I believe 270) packages, one of which, in an enormous case, was a perambulator (why could not such a thing have been got in Denmark? Kanne declaimed loudly against the nurses for having taken it), and consequently we did not reach our hotel (the Bristol) in Paris till about 9. Both the P. and Prss., I think, very much enjoyed their stay in Paris – Their great delight was to walk out shopping during the day, and to go to one or other of the theatres at night.

A most amusing incident happened to the Princess – She was shopping on foot in the Palais Royal, accompanied by Miss Vaughan, and had just left a shop, where she had been making purchases, when the shopwoman ran after her with a parcel which she said the Pss. had left on the counter. The Pss. did not recollect having done so, but not being sure took the parcel, and felt it to see what it contained. She thought it was a pair of slippers, but fancying rather an odd smell proceeded from it, she opened it and found it contained – a lobster!!!! At that moment the shopwoman came running back with many apologies to say the parcel belonged to another customer, who had come back for it. You can imagine the amusement of H.R.H.

I heard the Queen's not having returned the Empress's visit very much regretted in Paris, not that the Empress had minded it personally, (although she had expected a visit and had prepared flowers for the Q.) but it had given an opportunity to the enemies of the dynasty to say: – 'There you see the Empress is a parvenue, the Queen of England would not return her visit.' Then too I am told unfortunately the Q. (who could not return the visit on account of fatigue etc.) asked the Empress where she would recommend her to drive as she wanted to see a little of Paris; this to the Empress, who had come up to the Elysée Bourbon instead of the Tuileries, that it might be a less distance for the Q. to come and return the visit. Of course all this is only the gossip of the place, but it has no doubt a certain foundation in fact. The French were much displeased too at the Queen's not showing herself and at the gates of the Embassy being (contrary to their usual custom) kept shut. Minter who was there at the time heard some hisses and cries of 'A bas les Anglais,' as the Queen drove out.

The visit to Compiègne was a very pleasant one. The Emperor came himself to the station to meet the P. and Pss. (Her R.H. had never seen him before) and both he and the Empress accompanied them to the station on their departure – which was considered a great attention. Both the General and myself thought the Emperor looking much better than we had expected. Though he did not ride on the hunting day, he walked for four hours out shooting the next day, slowly he walks and is rather lame, but he did not seem at all fatigued afterwards, nor did his countenance nor his manner give one the idea of his being older than his real age (60). The hunting was rather a failure, as after the hounds had been once turned off we never saw them again. The accident which happened to the Prince was a very curious one, as he was galloping down one of the drives a stag happened to cross it and as neither had time to get out of each other's way a collision ensued and H.R.H. and his horse were knocked completely over, happily the ground was very soft and the allée on that place rather wider than usual, or a serious accident might have occurred. As it was the P. was a good deal bruised and was stiff for three or four days afterwards. In the evg. there was the curée, of *the* stag which it was *said* we had hunted, and which we had *not* seen killed – The sight was a very picturesque one, and exactly like the description which everybody has read of it. We dined (114 in number) in a long gallery, the cuisine was not good – for an Emperor's table – I thought perhaps it was because it was a jour maigre, but I was told it was much the same on other days. There was dancing after dinner till about ½ p. eleven o'clock and then to bed. For Ly. Augusta's information I will mention that both the Empress and the Princess wore dresses of green, but of totally different shades, and much to the delight of us English, the Pss. was incomparably the best dressed of the two. Ly. Carmarthen and I thought the French ladies did not turn out well, they wore some a profusion of colours, which did not harmonize well together, and their dresses appeared to be neither new nor fresh. The shooting the next day was a great success, very well managed and no butchery. We walked for two hours, then a dejeuner, and then 2 hours more shooting, never going twice over the same ground – 1469 head were bagged, of which the Prince of Wales killed the most, 270 head – The Emperor (who is not at all a jealous shot) coming off third but with 239.

We left Paris last Thursday evg. at 5, reached Cologne at 5 the next morning, remained there all day, starting again at 7.15 at night, and at 7 on Saty. morning arrived at Hohensdorf, where we had to get out of our carriage and cross the Elbe by a steam ferry through floating ice (pleasant, so early in the morning!) to Lanenburg, whence a very slow train brought us to Lubeck at 11. After breakfasting at the hotel we embarked on board a Danish Govt. dispatch boat, and after an hour and a half going down the Trave, 8 hrs. steaming brought us to Korsoer (we had a rapid rather roughish passage, both the P. and Pss. being ill): we remained on board the night, and landing the next day at 9.30 a special train brought us in 3 hrs. 96 miles via Copenhagen to Fredensborg. The Crown Prince came to meet the Prss. at Korsoer, and the King at Copenhagen. Her R.H. was very much cheered by the people. She looked so well and charming, and seemed so pleased and happy at getting home, that it did one good to see her. The great discomfort here is one's bed, which is too short, and the couvertures too narrow for one to tuck oneself in.

Today is the Princess's birthday, at one o'clock we all go to offer our felicitations – at 6 a grand dinner and in the evg. a dance.

Gulde Palads, Kjobenhaon.
Dec: 31.

. . . Thank you very much indeed for your most interesting letter of the 15th. . . . I was much struck by your account of the behaviour of Bright on taking the Affirmation. – I wonder if you agree with me in thinking that the greatest demagogues always show the most obsequiousness – Look at the Americans – Even here and at Stockholm I have noticed the different way in which the American Ministers bow to royalty from their diplomatic colleagues. To the one it seems natural and easy and gentlemanlike, in the other forced and obsequious.

Since I wrote the Prince paid a rapid visit to Sweden, leaving Fredensborg one Tuesday, and returning there the Wedy. week afterwards – It took us two days to get to Stockholm, sleeping at Toukoping – and 24 hours almost to a minute in returning, H.R.H. having taken an express train part of the way, otherwise in Sweden in winter the trains do not run in the night. The ostensible reason of the visit to Sweden was to shoot a bear, but owing to there being no snow there was no possibility of getting near Bruin. Everybody was very kind and hospitable and particular attention was paid to myself, as the only member of H.R.H.'s suite – The King I don't like; he is frank and open, a good musician and an accomplished painter, but he is not gentlemanlike, is too familiar with his subordinates. . . .

By the way, in Sweden when one is asked to take wine

with anybody, it is not only expected that you should
empty your glass, but also that you should invite a few
minutes afterwards the individual who has asked you, to
drink wine again with you. Of course Royalties are not
asked back, but they are expected to ask a good many
people to drink wine, and I was delighted that our Prince
came out of the ordeal triumphantly, always doing the
right thing yet never exceeding. His Equerry also was
never the worse. The Queen is very amiable, very ugly.
I liked her. The Princess (engaged to the Crown Prince
of Denmark) though plain, yet put me in mind of our
pretty Pss. Louise – She seemed intelligent and amiable,
spoke English remarkably well, and had very pleasing
manners with a degree of bashfulness suitable to her age
(16) – She is to be married in June or July. I may be
wrong, but I don't think the alliance is popular either in
Sweden or in Denmark – The two nations do not like
each other – and Danish is to a Swede as Portuguese
to a Spanish or (may I say) American to an Englishman.

The Prince was made a freemason by the K. of Sweden.
I am sorry as I think our Queen may not like it, and for
other reasons, which will probably occur to you, though
as I am not a freemason myself, I cannot tell how far the
objects of the society may be innocuous or beneficial.
Lord de Grey, I understand, approves of the P. becoming
one, and in Sweden.

I am summoned away so must conclude this with my
very kind remembrances to Lady Augusta.

In the meantime, Dean Stanley was using the impressions of his Irish tour in the cause of the coming election.
He had written a letter supporting the candidature of Mill

and he found 'Westminster all in a blaze' over his candour. Lady Augusta wrote of it to her sister.

'A. is much disgusted with the electioneering, the appeal to the passion, stupidity etc., on all sides – People are furious with him for his letter about Mill –

Later.

'Ly. Cranborne told A. that nothing could equal Dizzy's *lies.* – that Gladstone found out he meant to outbid him by bringing in a more sweeping Irish Reform – and hastened to gather his own party together by proposing his. – Goodness knows – everyone is of opinion that the most statesmanlike solution would be establishing all three bodies in Ireland – but they fold their hands and say *too late.* Some sort of Concordat to get a hold over the Catholics and a voice in the appoint. of their Bishops. – Prss. Helena was loud in her praise of Dizzy. He has got the length of their feet, but she quoted Genl. Grey also as saying his "letters were the most statesmanlike of any that he had seen for years!" – The Christians [Prince and Princess] sent on Tuesday to propose themselves to go over the Abbey and to Luncheon on Wedy. . . . were ill, so it made it rather difficult. But we had no one but them and they enjoyed it.

'In the evening A. and I went to Dizzy's reception at the F.O. and were fortunate enough to see D. and Mrs. D., escorting and escorted by the Pr. and Prss. of Wales, and followed by all the R. family!!!! It was funny. –

'On Thursday the Gladstones dined – the Greys and others, and Friday we dined with Css. Cowper and met them again – a most pleasant house, quite like a French small reception afterwards. Fridays and Tuesdays they

106

have dinners and their own set drop in. – quantities of chairs comfortably dotted about making up little knots.'

They also went to Germany before the end of the year and, towards the end of October, Lady Augusta wrote to the Queen, from Baden:

'Before leaving Baden, I venture to write these few lines to say that since our arrival on Friday we have seen dearest Princess Hohenlohe several times. . . .

'. . . We had a most exquisite week of almost summer weather for our travels till today, and have much enjoyed being here on the Birth Day of the Crown Prince and seeing the Princess and His Royal Highness and the two most prosperous little Children –[1] I quite look forward to Your Majesty's seeing the love of the darling little couple for One Another and their dear ways. – The little Princess seems to me to recall Prince Sigismund very much. – The Crown Princess looked very well and very charming yesterday evening, and the Crown Prince's military, becomes H.R.H. exceedingly. The King [William] looks so bright and so much younger since all these great events, that I could hardly recognise His Majesty – In conversation the King referred to that heart stirring evening in 48 when Your Majesty appeared with Him (the Prince of Prussia) at the Opera, and when Your Majesty's feeling and sympathy helped to soften the painful contrast of that reception, with the demonstrations in Berlin, the vivid recollection of which made His Majesty appreciate the outburst of loyalty all the more. – The Queen of Prussia has been, as always, most kind to us. – It always

---

[1] *Prince William, afterwards the Kaiser, and Princess Charlotte.*

107

warms my heart to see One who is so affectionately attached to Your Majesty. – The Grand Duchess of Baden [1] I had never seen before, and that has been a very great pleasure and interest. –'

[1] *Daughter of the King of Prussia.*

CHAPTER VI

The Queen and Ireland. Christine Nilsson, Lady Augusta, and the Dean. Consecration of Dr. Wordsworth as Bishop of Lincoln. The Queen meets Carlyle. Cardinal Manning in the House of Commons. The consecration of Dr. Temple as Bishop of Exeter. Dr. Hayman's unpopularity at Rugby. The Queen and Solomon.

CHAPTER VI

1869-70.

In February of 1869, Lady Augusta was summoned suddenly to Osborne.

'I was telegraphed for, having been obliged to own that I was quite well again. I went down the 12th and returned the 15th . . . H.M. was very kind and amiable. I *saw* none of the disagreeables, but have no hope of the ministers doing any good. She is quite satisfied with them and of course gives them every support, as she ought – but Genl. Grey was very angry with her about the Irish matters. She will not hear of anything but flying visits there for herself or any of the family. I believe she is so afraid lest any of them should be taken up by, or take up the Irish so as to throw Balmoral into the shade, now or later. I really do. She talks however of a visit to the places we described as being interesting. . . .'

She wrote to Madame Mohl on July 21st:

'I saw Nilsson [1] yesterday. She had called when I was

[1] The Prima Donna, Christine Nilsson, who was a frequent visitor to the Deanery. She was married at Westminster, and a nephew of Lady Augusta has recalled an amusing scene on her wedding day, when she came out from the service to the Deanery. He writes 'a very splendid, fair haired, voluminous lady, in a white satin dress, embroidered all over with roses and white silk, bursting into the drawing-room and throwing her arms around my poor little uncle's neck and

out and I called and found her resting before the opera and looking so pretty. She told me of her visit to Windsor which had enchanted her. The Queen came into the D. room. She had not heard music since the Prince's death and made her sing six songs. The Ct. and Cts. de Paris said She spoke with great pleasure of her afterwards. I hope I shall hear about it when I go to Osborne next week. Nilsson spoke so nicely – spoke of the Prince of Wales and all the bad stories she heard of him, but how very nice and gentlemanlike and respectful his manner was to her.

'I do not believe these stories a bit.

'She told me someone had remarked to her that she did not curtsey enough to the people – I patted her on the back famously when she explained that nothing would induce her to curtsey in the middle of her acting – to go out of her "rôle" and become Miss Nilsson in the middle, and then go on again. Do not you think she is right? It is remarkable to find so much dignity in a peasant girl.

'Yesterday was the Consecration of Wordsworth [1]– really a very fine and impressive and solemn service. – 150 Clergy and Bishops and 20 administering the Communion at one time. The congregation so large that the Service Communion and Consecration alone – lasted 4 hours. It was beautiful. The Members of Convocation had their red gowns and the lawn, etc., over them and the Archbishop had a chorister to hold his train as he

embracing him. The look of misery on his face, the way he shrivelled up was extraordinarily comic to see, and the scene has never faded from my memory.'

[1] *Wordsworth, who had been ardent in protesting against Dean Stanley's appointment to Westminster from the pulpit of the Abbey, was Consecrated as Bishop of Lincoln.*

walked up in procession – fancy Arthur arranging for such
a display of vestments!

'The music lovely. The first V. of the "new Creator"
by a single boy was too beautiful.

'The Wordsworths dined with us, a dinner of 22, and all
the friends and neighbours in the evening – most friendly
and charming it was. Pour tout dire Christopher Wordsworth kissed me!!!!

'Dear Wordsworth was very touching. He is narrow
and in some respects a fanatic – but he is a truly devoted
man and the numbers that flocked to the Service seemed
animated by his earnestness. . . .'

February 25.

'Pss. Helena's safe accouchement is a great matter over –
That particular business will not, we hope, change the
Queen's London plans – and as She thought the fate of
Nations depended on its being a Boy, I am glad it is. –
Tho' what shall we do with them later?

'H.M. has notified that she will come to 5 o'clock tea
here on the 4th, to meet (her own choice) the *Grotes*! –
Cha, Lyells, Browning and Carlyle!! [1] She has often talked

[1] The Queen recorded this meeting in her Journal, writing on
March the 4th: 'Drove to the Deanery at Westminster, where the
Dean and Augusta had invited the following celebrities to meet me:
Mr. Carlyle, the historian, a strange-looking eccentric old Scotchman,
who holds forth, in a drawling melancholy voice, with a broad Scotch
accent, upon Scotland and upon the utter degeneration of everything; Mr. and Mrs. Grote, old acquaintances of mine from Kensington, unaltered, she very peculiar, clever and masculine, he also an
historian, of the old school; Sir C. and Lady Lyell, he an old
acquaintance, most agreeable, and she very pleasing; Mr. Browning,
the poet, a very agreeable man. It was, at first, very shy work speaking to them, when they were all drawn up; but afterwards, when tea
was being drunk, Augusta got them to come and sit near me, and
they were very agreeable and talked very entertainingly.'

of such a scheme. I hope it will turn out well. Carlyle was going on in a way very edifying for her to hear, about the Prussians, when we went to invite him. A. hoped he might continue the topic. We must have him to meet you when you come here – he is too amusing and interesting. . . .

'A. is going on Monday to hear the bringing in of the Irish Bill. – they say Gladstone is to speak 5 hours! . . . Even among the Ministers, almost all agree that the plan is most objectionable, but you must keep the party together. Is it not funny?

'We have dined twice at small parties with the Gladstones – very amiable and agreeable – but he talked to A. of *everything*, but never a word on this subject, tho' he alluded to some minor thing in the pamphlet. . . . A. went to the first night debate in the Commons and the 2nd., and sat between Manning and Jeff. Davis!!! When Disraeli described the Established Church as a sort of refuge for those excluded by rigid sects or repelled by Rome, Manning asked satirically if that description he accepted – "As the description of the real *Evangelical Church.*"

' "Yes, for that was commissioned to seek and save the lost."

'Our Manning did not reply. A. thought Bright's speech the nearest thing to eloquence he heard.'

In September of 1869, Madame Mohl wrote from Paris:

'Dearest Dear, . . . Whether we are here or not, you will be more at home here than at an hotel; and Julie and I have settled you are to come to your room, and she'll put up new curtains, at which you are to fall into a syncope of admiration.'

Madame Mohl was then seventy-six – but she was undaunted and lively as ever.

Lady Augusta and the Dean arrived in Paris to find their old friend Père Hyacinthe, the Superior of the Carmelite Convent at Passy, excommunicated and on his way to America. They went to Munich, Rome, and Naples. He returned to England at the end of the year, to find the clergy in an uproar over the appointment of Dr. Temple as Bishop of Exeter. (Afterwards Archbishop of Canterbury.) Pusey said it was 'the most frightful enormity that has ever been perpetrated by a Prime Minister.'

Special arrangements for the forcible ejection of demonstrators had to be made at the Abbey, during the Consecration Service. So the Dean did not return to a peaceful regime, after his holiday abroad. Lady Augusta wrote to her sister:

'. . . We have been overwhelmed since our arrival on Wedy. evening – Never did there seem to be such an "avalanche" of distasteful questions ready to assail my poor, dear Arthur. His heart is so heavy. The trial is so very great, to him as a friend, a Churchman, an Englishman. The contrast to the joy of last year when in Paris we learnt the appointment, a joy and thankfulness which subsequent events have justified – so bitter, crushed by the sense of the loss so mysterious by the discouragement, as if Providence were almost against the Church he loves so well – but his faith and patience and sweetness are so beautiful – and only think what it is to find him assailed on his return by three sheets foolscap from Dr. Scott complaining of the place of the Masters in the Processions, etc., complaints of the vergers, taking money – endless squabbles, etc. It does make one's heart ache.'

Lady Augusta wrote of Dr. Temple that he

'is so calm and strong that he is very little troubled by all the attacks. The labour of answering the letters was almost overwhelming but he never had a doubt as to the only course he would and ought to pursue and therefore he had no agony of uncertainty, only the pain of refusing many who wrote in a "friendly" way and with true anxiety for the Church. Both at Chapel at Rugby and at the Consecration, he looked quite absorbed in the higher spiritual thoughts and communion – and one felt that, feeling as he was doing, the jarring of such interruptions must have been very painful at the time. What has really tried him to the utmost was the grievous disappt. about Rugby.[1] He had no idea that the Trustees, who had always supported and apparently trusted him, would dream of anything but getg. the best man, and when the appointment was announced, he was quite broken hearted. He and the Masters did not care in the least about the opinion of the Master, they would have quite

[1] This reference is to the appointment of Dr. Hayman as Head-master of Rugby, when Dr. Temple resigned to become Bishop of Exeter. Dr. Temple and the masters did not favour Dr. Hayman, for he came as a Conservative into a traditionally Liberal camp. During the four years he was at Rugby there was a great deal of dissension, and he was finally dismissed in December of 1873, by the governing body, which included his predecessor, Dr. Temple, and Dr. Bradley, formerly Assistant Master at Rugby, then Head-master of Marlborough and later Dean of Westminster.

understood a change being made as to political or theological views – provided they chose the best man of the
party. But the Masters and he himself cannot feel confidence in this man. Not his teaching, but his tact in
handling boys and his power of inspiring respect and confidence by his character.'

Lady Augusta to the Queen.
[From the published letters.]

Madam, – I am sure that Your Majesty will be pleased
to learn that all passed off well today. . . . The sermon
was much superior to what we expected, and very affecting from the real love and veneration for Dr. Temple.
. . . A stranger asked me, as we came out, who a lady
was, who had shown great emotion during the Service
and had wept bitterly. It happened to be Jenny Lind, but
I did not tell the name; I merely replied 'It is the Mother
of a Rugby Boy who knows what her Son is losing,' and
so it is. . . .

But there was one compensation in their return. Dean
Stanley's passion for the tombs of the great was the subject of much humour during the time he was at Westminster – indeed, his eagerness to claim the famous dead
for Westminster caused the Queen herself to call him
'that body snatcher Arthur Stanley.'
While he was on the way back from his holiday, with
all the news of Dr. Temple's appointment, Pusey's
vitriolic attack on him and the disagreeable details of
events at Westminster, Lady Augusta writes:

'A. has this one drop of comfort in returning home. A
Roman Sarcophagus has been found in the North green

117

close, under the Abbey walls – with a beautifully cut Latin inscription, the names of the dead person and those who erected the Mont. but with a cross carved in the lid of a later date.'

The New Year opened with Lady Augusta and the Dean at Westminster. On January 9th, she wrote to her sister:

'We went up on Friday to Lord Houghton's and met there Mr. and Mrs. Fred Harrison, he a prominent member of the comteish sect and a mad Frenchman. He did not think Père Hyacinthe nearly French enough, and he wishes the Government to enlist fifty thousand Irish to send to fight for the French – This he says wd. put an end to our "Irish difficulty." Mr. Froude hardly confirms this, for he says there was a great Fair in Kerry, just at the outbreak of the war and the people were so sure the English Government were French that, for one day, they were all enthusiastic Germans!!! . . . On Thursday we went to dear Victoria Welby's, such a lovely house – she is a delightful character. Père Hyacinthe came back last night, greatly pleased with Alnwick.' [1]

January 20, 1870.

'We had a splendid tea of over seventy vergers, the workmen, all the people of the Abbey and their wives and babies in the College Hall. I visited the choristers before and installed the elders in the music gallery from whence suddenly, before they began to eat, rose sounds of music – "God Save the Queen" – to the surprise and delight of the guests. The little choristers waited and the others sang

[1] *Where he had been staying with the Duke and Duchess of Northumberland.*

and then we had the magic lantern views of the East, explained by Arthur in the Jerusalem chamber. – All very nice. . . .

'The first impressions of Eton were favourable. J— and M— are to have the same room. J. was quite self-possessed and practical – enquired where he was to be examined and where he was to have tea and, when warned his books might be stolen by the old hands, he said "They are only lesson books – they will not take them, but I will lock up my ham and chicken" . . .'

Lady Augusta's papers include an interesting letter from Henry Ponsonby to the Dean, written on August the 20th of this year.

Windsor Castle.

My dear Dean,

I should not have troubled you with my views on Biblical revision had not the Queen urged me to ask your opinion on one point. The last letter from the Bishop of Gloucester was most interesting and he enclosed confidentially the printed sheet of what corrections have been proposed. Some of these, trifling as they seem to be, will produce a great deal of diversity of opinion.

I daresay you have seen the revised copy of the 3 first chapters of St. Matthew. My observation is solely confined to the Genealogical portion, where the well understood difficulty of alluding to Bathsheba, without naming her, has been got over, I can't help thinking, in a very odd way – 'David begat Solomon of her of Uriah' is rendered 'of the wife of Uriah.' Surely when this is so written, it proves Solomon to have been illegitimate – But in reality his mother was married to David – having been the widow of Uriah – for Uriah was dead when the first child was born. All this is clearly expressed in the Authorized Version by 'her that had been the wife of Uriah' and if it is necessary to change this, ought they not to say the 'widow' of Uriah? The Queen is rather scandalized by the proposed alteration – and wants to know what you think of it?

This I believe is nearly the only subject we have had much discourse on for the last 3 weeks, except the war which entirely absorbs our entire faculties.

Yours very truly,
HENRY PONSONBY.

Madame Mohl to Lady Augusta.

Paris, May 3rd, 1870.

I had a profounder veneration for the Duc de Broglie than for any one else, and though the habit was acquired only for three winters, it had taken great hold. I never could venture to go there since his death till last Sunday night, and then Albert seemed so cordial that I shall certainly go again, and perhaps keep it up. I went to thank him for coming with alacrity to a breakfast at ten! with Lord John Russell and his spouse. The hour was his (Lord R.'s) choice, and M. Mignet vowed he could not come out so early; but I had Guizot, Barthelemy, the Broglies, and M. de Parieu, a minister you don't know, but who often comes to see some of our exotics, which vegetable he has a great taste for, though a minister under this rascal-ocracy, I even invited him, because he has been known to speak very roughly to its chief. Though overwhelmed with business he came, and Lanfrey, whom I sat by Lord John at breakfast. My breakfast, though woefully managed in the creature comforts, had much success; but the best was this. At Lord Lyons', that dear man Lord John said to the Princess Julie (née Buonaparte), 'I was introduced yesterday to M. Lanfrey, a very clever young writer.'

Julie. 'What, the fellow who has written that abominable book?'

Lord Lyons came to the rescue to pacify her; but Lord J. Russell, nothing abashed, said, 'Oh, I liked him very much; he is very clever and very modest.' Was not that a tit-bit for you and me?

CHAPTER VII

The Franco-Prussian War. Lady Augusta and the Dean visit the battle-fields. Bismarck and the Emperor. The Crown Prince and the Princess Royal and the effects and opinions of war. Oberammergau. Wagner. The Old Catholics. Princess Alice and Princess Hohenlohe. Genoa. Rome. An abandoned audience with the Pope.

1870.

Lady Augusta was drawn into the excitement of the Franco-Prussian War with more than ordinary interest, and from the 18th of July in 1870, until peace was declared the following year, her letters are filled with opinions and announcements. There is an interesting note among her papers, written about 'The Tuileries on the evening before the Emperor's departure for the War.' . . . 'On the night before the Emperor left for the Army – all the family came to take leave at St. Cloud – The Empress was in the highest spirits – She said that Prs. Julie looked blank and seemed surprised and her sister said "pauvre femme, elle pense que si les premiers de St Cyr partent, son fils ne serait peutêtre pas loin des   " – "O quelle idée, si les premiers de St Cyr étaient appelés nous serions déjà bien malades" – "L'Empereur qui était très triste répondit doucement 'Vous avez raison ma Cousine, ce ne serait point impossible que l'on fît marcher les jeunes gens de St Cyr' " – "Ce n'est pas seulement un motif personnel qui me préoccupe, je songe a ce que doit être cette guerre à les deux cent mille hommes qui peuvent rester sur le ch: de bataille, vos frères apres tout." – "Ah par exemple, est-ce que par hasard vous allez appeler les Prussiens vos frères, vous?" – The Emperor spoke quietly on her side and kissed her tenderly twice as they parted, calling up her Son and Nephew to kiss them – "les baisers de ces Enfants me porteront bonheur." The Boys were so much moved that they begged to come into her carriage – "tenez, c'est vous qui avez raison, cela est bien triste." ' They could not go to the Continent in the autumn, so they went to Scotland, and to her home near Dunfermline. Through his wife and his love of Scott, Dean Stanley was filled with almost childlike enthusiasm for the history of the north. Lady Augusta's home was Broomhall, near the church where her ancestor, Robert the Bruce, was buried. It was to Broomhall that Thomas Lord Elgin brought many of the marbles from the Parthenon, and here, on the shores of the Firth of Forth, where every acre of ground has a story to tell, where the sounds are of the water on the shore and the thousands of birds in the trees, Dean Stanley continued his hunt for historical places, under the guidance of his wife.

They returned to the Deanery, and on January 23rd, 1871, Lady Augusta wrote to her sister:

'. . . Foolo Lothian came to me to get the Queen to ask the Emperor to let out the women and children from Paris – as if it were possible. I said "I will intercede with Gambetta to make peace. He is responsible." '

Christ Church, Oxford.
February 27.

'Thank God we may now believe that it is truly peace, but what a blessing – we have heard interesting things from Max Muller. He wishes the annexations could have been done without, but believes they could not now –

126

Later.

'It was rather difficult to find kind enough things to say of the French, especially after hearing Mr. Corbett's account of their conduct at the entrance of the Germans. He, with Oliphant and a number of other correspondents, watched it from Mrs. Morrit's [1] rooms. He saw the *Beautiful* bearing of *the* "Uhlan," who rode first and alone. . . . Their courage and good nature and absence of "fanfaronade" were wonderful – and the conduct of the French mob as wonderful the other way – scowling, hissing, making faces, almost killing any civilian or any woman they could get hold of, and flying like sheep before the least look of a soldier. They gradually came nearer and touched them and their clothes. The passive Germans smoking their pipes in perfect patience. . . . The second day the Parisians were becoming quite calm and not only approached, but talked to them and were delighted with the politeness of the German officers and their assurance of their respect for their opponents and their accounts of the disadvantages that caused the French defeats – want of generals and want of discipline.

'. . . To the F.O. in the evening. We also took Lord Houghton's daughter – to her first party. I pounded the Prince of Wales well with what I had just heard from W. Corbett and referred him to him for an account of the Entry! He gave no indication of his own sentiments and was very amiable – . . . I hear that the Rothschilds think nothing of the new indemnity which France will easily pay.'

[1] Mrs. Morrit and her sister were supposed to have been the originals of Minna and Brenda in Scott's *The Pirate*. Their uncle was Mr. Morrit of Rokeby, a great friend of Scott's. Mrs. Morrit married her cousin of the same name.

It was not until late in 1871 that they went abroad again – to Sedan, where they saw 'the little house where the Emperor of the French had his interview with Bismarck,' and then the larger Château of Bellevue where he made the final capitulation with the King. A woman who was present at the scene took them up the small back stairs, 'the same by which the Emperor and Bismarck had mounted,' into two very small rooms. Bismarck and the King had sat in one of the little rooms, at a table with two chairs. Afterwards they went out and sat before the house on two other chairs, one of which was taken away by Bismarck and the other by a Prussian officer.

The woman told Lady Augusta that Bismarck had ridden off, leaving the Emperor who stayed in the little room upstairs for three hours. She waited outside and heard him call 'entrez.' He was sitting at the table with his head between his hands and, the Dean's letter says:

'without ever looking up, ordered her to call one of the French Generals. The General came, and the Emperor received him in like manner, never raising his head. At 10 a.m. Bismarck returned "en grand tenue," with what she called the " huissiers de mort" – a troop like the Black Brunswickers – to escort him to the Bellevue Château. As he went out he gave her five gold pieces, which she has had framed and hung up; "Bon enfant," she said – the one only good word we have heard of the unfortunate Emperor of the French.'

At Strasburg, Lady Augusta saw the Cathedral and the Ruins and drove to call on a theologian in the neighbourhood.

'We knew him to be favourable to Germany but found

him cold. Suddenly his Wife who was hot, but in the other sense, left the room and we said how difficult the next few years would be. "Oh moi, je m'en arrangerai bien, mais voyez-vous dans les familles – vous avez dû vous apercevoir que ma femme voit autrement" – at this juncture she returned and he relapsed into his former meek condition!!! But the division of families must be terrible. – It will be a *most* difficult job and one can *hardly* believe that they will succeed in raising the good will of the masses. The Catholics are furious, having hitherto reigned supreme and being very backward and superstitious – Froschwiller is a Prot. Village. Roisch-soffen, next to it, is Catholic – the inhabitants of the former had to keep watch for a fortnight before the battles, against an attack from those of the latter, and again, after the proclamation of the annexation. Mm. de D. told me she was obliged to be a little less attentive to the German wounded than to the French, to shield her-self from suspicion – they were ready, the French, to accuse her at any moment of partiality – She and her boys were alone in the Château during the battle – in the cellars, till the fight passed on beyond, and the battle was actually lost. They told us a curious instance of the Catholic intolerance and backwardness – first they have steadily opposed education and encouraged all manner of superstitious practices. – C. D.'s first wife was a perfect angel, scarcely touching earth. In some place where he was Préfet they used to say "M. le Préfet n'est pas Pro-testant il a parlé du bon Dieu – mais Mme. quand elle est seule le Dimanche elle s'enferme pour adorer un *veau d'or*!!!"

'Her Brother was at a dinner of the Authorities at which

was a Priest. A splendid Turkey was served and someone lamented to M. le Curé that it should be Friday – "N'importe, je le baptise *carpe*," which he did and all partook!

'We decided to try and dine Pss. Hohenlohe [1] at Baden and left Strasbourg at 4.30, by a most tedious train, which only reached Baden at 8.30, leaving us no time for dinner. We flew to Her and found Her, as also Pss. Feo[dore]. She looks delicate, and very bad colour and shattered I thought, but as beloved as ever and very enthusiastic about the war. Pss. Feo's Step Son and Husband were there. She only wished her own two had been old enough! We remained till 10.45 and walked down to the Badische Hof where we got some cold chicken, all fires being out. . . .

'. . . Curnex in his folly, had put our cloaks into the luggage car and we were perished thro' the night – added to which all keys are carried off during the night, and it was only thro' the charity of a Gentleman in uniform that the für Damen was kindly opened at sunrise at Darmstadt!! – At Frankfort, as I was tidying myself after this uncomfortable night, Prince Teck appeared at the window. He was accompanying the Queen of Denmark. . . . I think he must have found the ladies dull for he was quite tender to us.

'. . . We came on at noon to Potsdam – The carriages met us at the station and the beloved Princess [the Princess Royal] at the door – We had splendid and most comfortable rooms – nice fire to welcome us – had supper in our sitting room. Then they came to see us, and bed. I arrived still in my cotton frock which looked quite tidy and owing to which, and my juvenile hat, I was taken at

[1] *Queen Victoria's half-sister.*

Strasbourg for Arthur's daughter!! and systematically called Fräulein all along.'

In Potsdam they stayed with the Crown Prince and the Princess Royal at the Neue Palais for three days. The Crown Prince stood at the door. 'Immediately he showed us into a suite of splendid rooms on the ground floor,' wrote the Dean. The Crown Prince took them to their suite. 'In this room I was born and here many of your countrymen have slept before.' The paper on the walls was of painted peacocks.

Lady Augusta wrote:

'At 9. we breakfasted with the Pr. and Pss. and family and dined at 2 with them – supper with the whole party at 7.30 or 8. After breakfast we walked and drove and drove again and had tea out somewhere in the afternoon, spending much of the intervening time in the Pr's rooms – We quite overwhelmed him with questions about the war – his patience is inexhaustible and his sentiments on that as on all other subjects, making one long to hug him. May God preserve and guide him. . . .

Later.

'Nothing could be kinder than the Pr. and Pss. only giving us too much of their time – we felt we must propose to leave on Saturday out of discretion as they were to leave for Wilhelmshohe today. She was a little more distrait than in London, not having been well and the Baby being still very poorly – they fancied the water and air at P. had disagreed with them all, after their return from England, and had with much difficulty got the Emperor's consent to their moving to W. for change. He hates these moves. . . . I wish some of his ideas could be transplanted! He is, as to business, the slave of his Minister and goes to B. every day from Potsdam when there!! The Children were most tender to us – so delightful to talk to, so bright and interested in everything. Pr. William [afterwards the Kaiser] is a darling – the two youngest (but one) are rather unruly, but fine children – P. Vlademir very shy, however after some running up and down with Arthur, he quite took to him, calling for him – *Dim* – It was most amusing in our walks to see them all clustered round him.

'The Pss. has made a nice garden and a farm and dairy and arranged the village School and the Ch. Yard and left her mark everywhere –

'We had a sort of party at the evening meal on Thursday. . . . That evening meal is horrid, beginning with tea and cake and then meat – if only one might reverse it. On Saturday they had a great dinner for the Bavarian Officers of the Prince's Regiment at two – the Pss. decolletée – I in my blue, after that I packed and redressed and drove with Her, the Prince going to dine out again with the Guests somewhere at a military party!! We had tea and at 7 we left for [Berlin]. The Princess told us of one of the French Prisoners whom she asked if he had written to his Mother. "Non." – "Mais ne serait-elle pas inquiète?" – "Comment voulez vous, puisque j'étais pêcheur et qu'elle me voyait tous les jours partir pour la Mer elle devait bien s'attendre qu'un jour je ne reviendrais pas!!!" –

' "Avez vous une femme?"

' "Non, je promène ma petite peau toute seule a travers l'Europe." She said one day to a wounded one – "Vous paraissez bien aujourd'hui" –"Oui on me trouvait même

très bien autrefois" – Some Pss. Cousins of the Prince went
to visit and take gifts to the prisoners – who recd. them
most gratefully – but when out of sight but not yet out of
hearing – they exclaimed "Mon Dieu sont-elles laides!"
One of the Pss. told this herself with delight – The Turcos
had been told they wd. be killed if taken – hence their
furious attack on Ds. etc., they could hardly be made to
believe the contrary and when they did, many asked to
remain in Germany – One young one of 18 at Worth
who had 16 wounds recovered as by miracle. He adored
the Soeur who nursed him – "Moi guéri, moi marier
Sora – emmener Sora à Paris voir *Grand Monde*" – this
was discovered to be the *Cafés Chanteurs*.'

During the days they were at Potsdam, they walked
with the Crown Prince and Princess after breakfast.

'The battlefields furnished endless topics of conversation
with the Prince. No one could be more modest or frank
about them . . . one morning, in this walk, the whole
account of the triumphal entry was given by the children.
'Little Prince William rode in with his uncle, the Grand
Duke of Baden. "The Emperor stood for two hours in the
sun without his hat. And he is seventy-three! What do you
think of that?" "The flowers came sailing down from the
third and fourth storeys of the houses, so that at last you
could not see anything of the soldiers but their bayonets."
'It is impossible to write all the little anecdotes, etc.,
which make up the charm of a visit like this. I return,
however, to the thought that if monarchy is to be saved
by any man in this century, it will be by our host.'

In Berlin, Lady Augusta went to the Cathedral

'and heard a good sermon and much lovely singing – a choir of men unaccompanied, singing the Psalms of Mendelssohn. – I never heard anything more beautiful – the Church very full – a few remained for the Communion – a very simple service with more of these lovely chants. – We afterwards went to see Anna Helmholz – She was away – Her poor Boy is the same and the Babe is far from strong. – It looks all head – She is very uneasy – very dear. Pines a little for Heidelberg. . . . Anna H. says she is afraid that a small proportion of the officers did take things. . . . The dear old King has heard such rumours and is very miserable about it; but they try not to let him believe it. – On the whole however, this million of men have behaved admirably, and Anna says that you hear always "here we have nothing to complain of, but somewhere else they did so and so." There was nothing to be had in the villages and they, very hungry, could scarcely believe that nothing could be had – but generally they were on excellent terms with the peasants and townspeople. G. Busen marched into Pont a Musson with a Saxon Regt. and when he halted he heard a Private ask a Frenchman standing by "pourriez-vous m'indiquer un bon Libraire ici?" – At Charlottenburg I heard two privates saying rather contemptuously "Aber Compiègne ist viel schöner" –'

Their next journey was to see the Passion Play. They drove past

'beautiful hills and valleys, ever more exquisite than I can describe – the blue outline sharp and fanciful to a degree and ever varying – the rushing river, the dark woods and bright green meadows, here and there violet with colchicum flower – as someone said, like the reflection of the dark blue hills. . . . As we advanced we heard the tinkling of the bells as the herds of lovely cattle came down from the high pastures and ever again, the sounds of some church bells reached us, as we approached a village.

'Before we arrived at the foot of the steep hill, which leads up to the plateau on which Oberammergau stands, – the moon had risen in unusual brightness, the crowds thickened and by the time we reached "Unterberg" I can hardly describe what it was – every sort of thing on wheels, and every sort of creature on legs drawing it – immense long haycarts with awnings tightly drawn over them, stuffed with people . . . horses staggering, men calling out, four thousand people I believe, struggling to get away. We walked up the hill, through the thick wood, the moon dimly lighting our steps, and gradually, as we emerged from the crowd, the world relapsed into silence and nothing was heard but the rushing of the river at the bottom of the gorge. At length we gained the summit. We drove to the Burgomeister's . . . the morrow's play had only been announced three hours before, in consequence of the King's having intimated that he would be present . . . the good Burgomeister promised us five beds. . . .

'We breakfasted and welcomed another fine morning and off we went. . . . The guns fired and in walked the King,[1] accompanied by a brother of Prince Louis of Hesse. He is certainly a fine looking and handsome man, but he has such a very strange look in his eyes that I did not think him quite what I had expected of beauty. He sat in wrapped attention all the time, without his hat, tho'

[1] *Later the 'Mad King of Bavaria.'*

135

it was cold. The attendance was small, but one could think of nothing but the scene itself and I felt it to be all that it had been described and much more, for the individual impression is something quite different from any that words can convey. I quite yearn to see it again and again, to be able to dwell more on each successive thought and impression and to escape the distraction which the novelty and the fear of losing any part causes. . . . A. went down to the front row when it advanced, to hear better, and after the midday interval I joined him there. . . .

'After a walk late in the evening, we called on Ly. Franklin who was present and went with her to see Meyer who takes the principal part, and Pilate, who was the Christus in 1850. The first is a very solemn, quiet, thoughtful man, feeling the honour and dignity and sublimity of the task he had accepted. A very religious minded man. The other an excellent man also, but a thorough peasant and one could hardly believe that he, a few hours before, represented the Roman Governor with such dignity and high breeding and historical fidelity. . . . Pilate's two daughters personated, one the Virgin, the other one of the Guardian Angels in the choir. The latter is *beautiful* – and has been told it in every tone – but she cleans the boots and does the housework just the same and is as simple as ever. . . .'

They left Oberammergau in the morning and travelled to Munich, where they saw the procession 'for the opening of Reichstag which Pr. Luitpold opened. . . .'
Lady Augusta was fashionable enough not to accept Wagner unconditionally, and when she was in Munich, she went to see

136

'the "Walkure" and tho' at one moment I thought I must have been nearly maddened by the noise of all those screaming people, shrieking at the same moment, I was on the whole more pleased and able to appreciate it than I had expected at a first hearing. . . .

'Did I tell you of my being admitted with another lady "connected with the press" to the Alt Katolik [1] meeting on Saturday. *No ladies* are allowed to be present at what can be looked upon as a political meeting in Bavaria and an infraction of the law might at any moment cause a meeting to be broken up. We were put into a sort of tent into which passers by were continually endeavouring to penetrate. We were 4, and at each attempt we put an extra pin to fasten it. At last it was like a pin cushion! I leave you to imagine how terrified I was and *what* the intruders must have taken it for! – There were very fine speeches – P. Hyacinthe's most eloquent and beautiful – He spoke on Monday, to Ladies only, and he said – but this is only for yrselves, for it is as if A. had said it, so unusual with him, "Elles sont mises comme des *cuisinières*, mais *comme* elles sont *intelligentes*" – The Meeting has been a great success. . . .

'Sir R. Blennerhassett says it is astounding how these diplomats know so little and surround themselves only by their Brother diplomats – not caring to cultivate the intelligent people of the Country – The King is far from ultra-montane – is liberal and intelligent, but he is

[1] The Old Catholics were formed as a result of the loss of the Pope's temporal power and the proclamation of the dogma of infallibility. These two events aroused the German Roman Catholics, and the Liberals among them, repudiating the dogma, formed themselves into a separate body, the Old Catholics, with the excommunicated Dr. Döllinger as leader.

strange and capricious, lives apart and can not be brought to carry on things consecutively. – Old King Louis has a sister who writes tracts and is excellent and distributes them to the soldiers – but is quite cracked on several points – the King is outwardly her image!'

Oct. 9.

My own,

We are sleeping here at the 3 Kings with the Rhine flowing under our windows – I told you that Max [Müller] and we drove with dear Alice on Saturday, the Gentlemen returning on foot – in the mng. we had been with P. Alice at 9.30 and walked with her and L. till she met her Brothers – and again we went to the station to see them off – only to think of the two dear sweet Princesses coming – and that horrid Manchester appearing in colors! – The Duchess of Hamilton, her daughter and the lovely Boy were also there and dear 'Uncle Gustaf' who always remembers Arran! – Pr. A. spoke much of the delight of having Victoria [1] as a friend and companion for her – She will adore the Baby – such a bright darling I never saw . . . then I went to the Empress and attended on Her to the English Church, which made me feel very shy. – She was very kind and almost wound up with me after, as she said when the Emp[eror] arrived, all Her habits had to change. – At 4 we went with the little Mulhes to see Him arrive and He looked young and well and bright and simple – I thought they [the Children] behaved so well – were so nice in feeling and sentiment and in good sense –. . .

[1] *Victoria Baillie, daughter of Lady Augusta's sister, afterwards the Hon. Mrs. Alaric Grant.*

They quite put me in mind of Her in their prompt, quiet, tender, thoughtful, practical way of doing all things. . . . Poor things, it was trial enough to feel, how little the beloved could have them with Her – in those stations, so little can be done for one another – and that the servants become necessary and intimate and indispensable as they would not otherwise – On Sunday Max and Mrs. [Müller] dined with us, a sort of table d'hôte in the Andrews' rooms, so pleasant and they all enjoyed it –

. . . Pss. A[lice] and Pr. Victor went to — the day before. She was so charming on Monday – she and Pss. Ada came by appointment at 4 and I gave them tea and we had a long talk – and I spoke to Pss. Hohenlohe of all the dear Baroness [Späth] [1] used to describe of Her Father – and his chivalrous truthfulness and sense of honor and how that had been the characteristic of all the family. – Her eyes filled with tears and she seized my hand and said – 'that is what makes me so happy – I know that, I feel that for my Children – and I should not be so happy a Wife if my Husband were not what He is, in all the other relations of life – such a Son as he has been – and O what a loss to Him,[2] he could ask her, tell her everything.' It was very sweet. Dear Pss. A. also and so so sad. Her Husband had to go home. She *adores* Him. – I will report on their *worth* and *truthfulness* and high mindedness to the Queen. They have at least that of their Parents, and modest – I told you how happy a thought struck me of offering to go to Miss Bartlett in the evg. and how we had such a charming talk with the Gd. Duchess of Baden – so charming and interesting – and it was quite

[1] *Lady-in-waiting to the Duchess of Kent.*
[2] *His mother was dead.*

a chance for she left next morning at 10. She said Miss B. might come to me before and so she did at 9, on Her way to the Empress – very alarming but she is much bolder now and the Empress said after, of the two, she preferred too retiring to too pushing! Mr. de Guson wanted me to go with them to the Opera but I was rather disinclined, however the Empress sent for us to come just at the time, at 7 yesterday and was very amiable, but we had not any very 'suive' conversation with Her because she said the Emperor wished to see us and in He came looking quite as brisk as ever, but his face rather more thin and worn and aged. He spoke with his whole heart about the beloved One The Queen and quite shewed that He appreciated Her. He had been to see the poor desolate House (and had shewn much feeling) where he said He so much enjoyed going and conversing with Her on all subjects. She was 'si bien orientée' on all and Her judgement was so right and Her feeling so true and she was so good. It was pleasant to hear Him, dear old Man. We spoke to Him of the battles and He said what terrible sights those were – but when one thought one was in the right, and war was begun, one must go on to make an end and the devotion of soldiers and people shewed it was a righteous cause – and above all, the blessing from above which was so evidently with them, and without which, their arms could not thus have triumphed. 'Oui nous avons un Allié là-haut – sans Lui nous étions rien' – Nobody who heard Him could ever have doubted the sincereness of the expressions in the Bulletins – He may not always be consistent but sincere he is. – The Duchess [Dowager] of Hamilton[1] I went to see – she was friendly, did not know

[1] *A Princess of Baden, married to the Duke of Hamilton.*

much of what had happened these last 9 years in England but asked about Mary L. Lady Elgin and said how much she would like to read the Memoir. And the Children – I felt quite shy of telling Her how blessedly they were turning out. She spoke of the war and how she loathed the French for their ingratitude to the Emperor – blamed the Empress but excused Him and said that the fine honorable high minded officers there, were nearly broken hearted at the conduct of the others and the troops. . . . She said as soon as they were on parole, the most of them they sent for the cocottes from Paris and General Weinssen took a Villa near Stuttgart where he entertained a famous one – She maintains all this to be true – I did not ask if the Emperor did the same – She saw him 4 days after Sedan, terribly cast down and again in Nov., by accident, meeting the Empress there. – She hopes he will never think of going back. –

Lady Augusta's next letter was written from Genoa, where they 'had an adventure' during the night.

'After our long weary journey, suddenly I was roused by a mouse running about me and my terror was only exceeded by Arthur's! The enemy went to the end of the room, where we supplied him plentifully with old rolls out of A.'s pockets, and where he kept up a jumping, screaming and noise that made us believe he must have been a rat! The people very frankly said they had many mice and set a trap in the morning.'

Dean Stanley could not

'be made to understand the Jesuit power, or to approve of their expulsion. M. de Circourt gave a most lurid explanation of it by saying that in the same way as gambling houses were forbidden and closed as public dangers, so should Jesuit establishments and their promoters be expelled. He almost wept as he described the ruin they wrought among the young generations in France.'

They went to Tivoli:

'The whole campagna bathed in a sea of gold and crimson, St. Peter's standing out alone like a hill in the distance – and in the foreground Tivoli with its waterfalls and rocks and picturesque walls and buildings – its broad green and its groves of trees, hundreds of years old.'

But they dined at a 'more than homely inn' and soon slept sound on beds 'the least downy possible.'

The Italian papers published a report of the fact that 'il padre Arthuro Stanley' had attended the Ald Katolik conference in Munich. And on the heels of the report, the proposed visit of the Dean and Lady Augusta to the Pope 'fell through' because of the Pope's strong feeling against the 'Anti-infallibilists.'

Lady Augusta to her sister.

Rome, Oct. 23.

We went over the Vatican Garden yesterday with which we were delighted – but pretty as it is, it makes one sad for the Pope who so enjoyed his drives, to know him deprived of them. Altogether it makes me very sad indeed to think how painful it must be to them all and to be so near it all thro' the telescope is in some respects more trying than to be away altogether – but the Pope looks well and is very cheerful I am told and receives a great many people. We met some who had been at a reception the other day when a purse was presented to H.H. by some Nuns and a very pretty sight it was and very pretty things the Pope said to them. If I was to choose a prison it should be the top of the Vatican certainly, for example the rooms of Antonelli – Ld. Howard told us a most excellent thing of an attack made on an Irish Monk by some rascally people in the Street. He was a newcomer and a true Irishman and he took up a chair or something handy and swung it round, causing the ruffians to take to their heels double quick – crying out 'Dio che Frate.' Do tell Miss Wyse, I was so pleased and dear Howard told it with something of the old Guardsman's spirit remaining still. –

They returned to England, travelling through Paris and staying there with Madame Mohl, to whom Lady Augusta wrote, on arrival in London:

November 11th.

'. . . The journey seemed like an afternoon expedition, for we lunched with you and supped in the library at eleven. It was two before A. had unsealed the most pressing of his letters, but he was none the worse. . . . Our breakfasts here have been a little disturbed by our indignation at the mean, base, stupid attacks on the Queen and the monarchy, delivered by Sir Charles Dilke, before a Newcastle audience. He is the author of a book called "Greater Britain" which had the success usually achieved by charlatans. Mr. Musgrave, late Governor of Vancouver Island, which Sir Charles professes to describe, told us that if his other assertions and pictures were as accurate as this, we might save ourselves the trouble of perusing the rest of his contributions to history. . . .'

CHAPTER VIII

The Prince of Wales' illness. The death of Lady
Charlotte Locker. The Dean and Lady Augusta
in Germany. Trèves and Aix. Death of Princess
Hohenlohe. The Queen's grief. Lady Augusta and
the Empress.

K

CHAPTER VIII

1871–2.

Towards the end of the year of 1871 the Prince of Wales fell ill of typhoid fever, and the letters to and from the Deanery speak of little else but the fears at Sandringham. Almost every day, letters or telegrams carried the bulletins to Lady Augusta. Lady Macclesfield wrote on December the 5th, when he was proving 'an excellent patient':

'The dear Princess keeps up with unshaken patience and courage. She is with the Prince all day long, and does *everything* for him – the fact of being able to do so, and of his preferring her ministrations to those of all others, has been her *best comfort* – or in her own words "my only comfort," and her sweetness of temper, and consideration for others has been unfailing –'

On the 10th, the Duchess of Roxburgh did not 'feel there is any hope,' and on that day Lady Augusta wrote to her sister:

'This dreadful news on Friday knocked us down – knowing they would have left Windsor, we drove to Victoria Park Station where the Queen was to change engines in order to hear something from her attendants. The D. of Edin. came while we were waiting – terribly overcome when we asked the nature of the attack. He

147

could only point to his chest and burst into tears. On Tuesday the Drs. had said all was going quite well and since it had been quite favorable. We saw the Duchess and Col. Ponsonby – she quite hopeless – I just caught a glimpse of the Queen as she arrived. She looked so small and miserable – poor poor thing – I was afraid she might have been vexed at our coming, but it touched her. . . . I am so thankful that the Princess finds her presence and sympathy a comfort. – The Dss. telegraphed on arriving that both showed wonderful fortitude – I cannot describe all Ly. Macclesfield says of the Princess – At one moment, poor little thing, she ran out in the dark to pray in the Church for a few minutes, to compose and strengthen herself. Is it not touching –'

On the 14th:

'The Queen was allowed to go up to his bed – he did not quite know her at first – but soon did and said he was glad to see her – She was in his room nearly the whole day, and sat a long time by his bed holding his hand –'

On December 15th, Lady Augusta wrote to her sister:

'You are by this time rejoicing with us – I can hardly keep my hope below confidence for the dear Patient has shewn such a good will to recover – such a strong constitution and has all along continued those encouraging symptoms of being able to eat – that I can but rejoice and anticipate good. Then all the outside Drs. have said so emphatically, first, that time was everything, then sleep, then any change for the better, however slight. – O what a rebound one's heart makes – only one is awed by the feeling shewn and by the call that feeling makes on him, who is the object of it. – May He rise not only from his sick bed, but to the height of His Mission – I *believe* He desires to do it – may God grant Him strength and grace, – Ly. Macclesfield spoke of His astonishing kind heartedness and consideration – never an unkind thing or word, in the family the same. – . . . How it touches one to read of the poor dear Queen sitting holding the P. of W.'s hand! Is it not affecting? I quite long to see Her thus, Her best self, by being taken out of herself – taken out of Doctors and maladies (I mean her own) and nerves and fighting off what Her own righteous conscience tells Her would be right. – I have your two dear letters Tuesday evening and Thursday morning – what a comfort to have that blessed Gd. Duchess [of Baden] and to know such a Being.'

Sunday, Dec. 17.

My darling,

After the happy bulletin of the morning we went to Clarence House to see the D. of Edin. who had just arrived and Oh! the delight of seeing the change in His face – He was almost ashamed of ever having doubted that His dear Brother would recover! but He explained that the sudden bad news that Friday, and having seen Mr. Birch bathed in tears, had unnerved him!! He described to us how on the morning of the 13th at 5., Gull sent for Him to consult as to whether he should not at 6 issue an extra bulletin stating that the strength was failing – The Duke begged him to wait but then he almost gave up hope – when presently there came some indication of a willingness to take nourishment and he heard in the Prince's own natural voice 'that's right *old Gull* –

that's good, two or three more spoonsful old Gull' – The epithet applied to a new acquaintance shewed that he was not quite himself, but he was so, in expressing his wishes and in the tone of his voice. By 8. the bulletin was issued and there was no decrease of strength to be chronicled – I imagine that the 36 hours of the wildest, loudest, incessant talking, in all languages – whistling, singing, began to subside about that time. – He described this phase as too terrible – but he does not think, except occasionally in the struggle for breath, that there was much conscious suffering. It was most touching to hear Pr. Alfred speak of Him with such love and admiration, almost with tears in his eyes, he spoke of his wonderful kindness and courtesy and consideration for every one, even in his wanderings – thanking for everything done for him and apologising when he recognised the Queen, kissing her hand and thanking her for coming etc. – He told us of his astonishing strength at one of the worst times as to exhaustion, he had raised his head and arranged his own pillows – on Friday I think, when still wandering, he suddenly took all his pillows one by one and threw them about the room – one at the Princess! not in anger, but just those funny things people do. – They think he knows how very ill he has been, not only from what he said to the Queen, but from the way he speaks of Dr. Gull whom he supposes to have been at death's door and recovering when almost despaired of!! Pr. A. spoke with the greatest enthusiasm of Dr. Gull – such courage, judgement, firmness, He said he never saw. Pr. Alfred takes great credit to himself for having suggested the pale ale on Wedy. which seemed to revive him so much – The P. of W. asked who had thought of it, and was told.

'That was a good idea of his but won't it make me too fat!!!!' –

The dear Princess is wonderfully well and all is lost in the sense of her present joy and thankfulness. He generally knew her and called her often by Her pet name 'and was she not happy then' added Pr. A. –

. . . One must be thankful for the Queen's complete happiness with the Prss. of W. and that part of the family. . . .

Wednesday, Dec. 20.

. . . I found yr. dear letter of the 17. on my return – O indeed may the Prince rise to all we should wish, with all that is in Him of good. – . . .

The Argylls were in Church on Sunday and we had tea with her on Monday – She looks very well and spoke with infinite love and admiration of Pss. Louise – Thinks she has so much in her and that She has a feeling of what is right – They lamented Gladstone's not understanding the Queen – he had pressed her, if she felt the sympathy to show it, by opening Parlt. or attending a Thanksgiving Service, or both – They thought he ought to let things come from Herself, as She felt able, and what she felt able for – the opening of P. being so especially trying – I have no doubt he is 'gauche' but I must say I honor him for pressing her duty on her – And Oh! that she should at this moment resent it! Poor poor dear!

Madame Mohl had stayed in England for many months during the Franco-Prussian War. Lady Augusta and the Dean had taken her back to Paris, whence she continued her letters to Lady Augusta. In January of 1872, she wrote:

'. . . Do you know the American ambassador here, and are you en mesure to give me a letter of introduction to him? I need scarcely say "don't do it," if it cannot be done with that grace and ease that you put into all your efforts to oblige, because I know your tact and wisdom, which make you so delightful to deal with. . . . We are pretty comfortable as far as mere living goes. Everything is much dearer; but our losses have been far less than I expected, and the wonder to me is, that after such a dreadful year, such a dreadful waste of life and means, such sums to be paid – first to the enemy, and next for the extravagances of the imperial government – that things are as good as they are. Such a waste of the poor animals – the cattle so diminished in number that my London kitten won't lap milk, forsooth, because it is so different from what she had at Florence Nightingale's. She goes about mewing for better, which they call cream.'

Lady Augusta replied in February:

'I am nearly quite well. . . . I caught cold originally, most appropriately, at the lecture on the Flood (from the Assyrian inscription) and in some way it took possession of me. . . . [Arthur] has had a week of fighting with Convocation. Sometimes he seems almost cast down by the stupidity and perverseness of men. He gave a sort of wail this evening, but is now dining at the club. . . . I should like to hear M. Mohl's comments on the New Bill, the Irish University from which *modern history* and modern philosophy are to be excluded. One would think that Mr. Gladstone came from the Emerald Isle himself, with such an invention.'

Lady Augusta wrote to her sister:

'We are so glad to be asked to Osborne the first Sunday of his [the Prince of Wales] being there. It will naturally give the opportunity A. wished for, but which he could hardly make otherwise.

Later.

'We had a lovely bright day for our journey to Leeds. At Peterborough, I suddenly saw Moodey [her maid] leading about a little girl of six or so, and on approaching I found that the little creature had her name and address sewn on to her! She had been sent in care of the guard and had fallen into the kindly hands of Moodey. She was very silent but gradually displayed all her possessions – new flannel petticoat and with much hilarity. . . .

'Before reaching Newcastle we were asked at several stations whether Mr. O'Sullivan was in the carriage, which he was not. At Newcastle a tremendous cheering greeted our arrival. This turned out to be the welcome for the missing man, no other than the champion of "Home Rule." The station master was furious. I said "I did not know you had so many Irish here." "They are English jackasses I am sorry to say." . . .

'Did I tell you how good the poor Wales boys were at dinner – no noise or fuss of directions about them – I congratulated their poor father – he said' he thought it very happy not to have to be always at them. "We were perhaps a little too much spoken to and at – at least we thought we could never do anything right anyhow." '

No record of family friendship is more lovely than the story of Lady Augusta, her sisters and brothers. Their father, Lord Elgin, had not left them at all well off. Their mother, the Dowager Lady Elgin, lived and died in Paris,

and the brothers and sisters were united by an extraordinary unselfish desire, each for the other's good. Personal humility and family loyalty were the characteristics
of all of them and, as all seven achieved definite success
and a degree of fame, they were all united by wide and
important interests. Lord Elgin, the eldest brother, had
died while Viceroy of India, General Bruce died of the
illness he contracted while travelling as Governor of the
Prince of Wales in the East, Sir Frederick Bruce served
as Minister in Pekin and died as British Minister in
Washington. The last brother, Thomas, was still alive.
He had been offered a peerage but, as a facetious reason
for refusing, he urged that he had only a house in London
and that he would accept the honour only if they made
him 'Lord 42, Hill Street.' But the three sisters were
bound together through the successive tragedies which
robbed them of their mother and three brothers. Lady
Frances Baillie was living in Carlsruhe, and Lady Charlotte Locker was in London. In April of 1872, the tie was
broken through the death of Lady Charlotte.

'She literally fell asleep, without a pang or a groan,'
wrote Lady Augusta. ' . . . It is very difficult to face this
separation. God only knows what she has been to each
and all of us in every circumstance of life. Oh, that
inexhaustible fountain of love, of helpfulness, of cheerfulness, of thoughtfulness for others, those brilliant gifts,
that understanding of everything and never failing sympathy and total absence of self. . . . Dearest Madame
Mohl, I do not like to sadden you, but it is *such* a comfort
to talk to you of Her, for I know how you loved and
appreciated Her and how you understand the life bond

that united us, never showing for a single instant by any word or thought or deed – even during the very trying illness, there has not been an instant of physical irritation – nothing but love and sweetness and patience and thankfulness.'

Towards the end of 1872, Lady Augusta and the Dean went to Germany. From Aix la Chapelle, Lady Augusta wrote to her sister. They had travelled

'on the trails of poor Louis XVI and his lumbering Berline. At St. Meinhauld we left the train and began to follow, step by step, Carlyle's description. You cannot think how breathlessly interesting it was. . . . We reached Varennes at 1 p.m. and as you may believe, well cross questioned every creature. The houses, the rooms, all are changed, but the outside. Localities tell the story in the most thrilling way. One sees where the Choiseul horses were expected to be and were not. And then, when they were a few hundred yards off, at the foot of the village and over the little bridge – quite unconscious. Carlyle only makes the mistake of saying they were in the *upper* room instead of the *lower*.'

They continued their journey and at Trèves they found that the 'Roman remains are the chief interest.' They took home 'a trophy of interest of another sort – two pebbles from the place where St. Athanasius sat and where he did *not* write the creed!'

At Aix they found the

'beautiful and curious Cathedral is being terribly spoiled, alas by ruthless restorers. Fancy their *painting* the fine early English granite pillars a sort of grey and all the roof

155

with little bunches of flowers, like an ugly room paper. I am afraid it is the Chapter.'

On Thursday the 19th of September, they were in Cologne, and then, within a few days, they were drawn to Baden to the death-bed of Princess Hohenlohe.

The Princess had withdrawn from English life, and the fact that she was Queen Victoria's half-sister is not generally remembered.

Her death in Baden stirred the earliest memories of the Queen. The half-sisters lived as children at Kensington Palace with their mother. Leigh Hunt writes of a day when he saw the little Princess Victoria 'coming up a cross path from the Bayswater gate, with a girl of her own age at her side, whose hand she was holding as if she loved her.' This was Princess Feodore who married Prince Hohenlohe and returned to the life of a small German Court.

A telegram from Queen Victoria brought the first news of the Princess's illness to Lady Augusta. With the Dean she hastened to Baden, too late,

'the light gone from those glorious eyes, the loving welcome, the bright kindling response silent,' Lady Augusta wrote to the Queen from Baden. 'The only sister and such a sister! A life long love and tenderness and sympathy and support which nothing on earth can ever replace. Dearest, dearest Madam, my own sore aching heart aches for Your Majesty with an unspeakable bitterness. . . . Yesterday afternoon Her Highness recognised and distinguished the Empress's voice downstairs at the entrance and roused Herself to see Her.' Later: 'the lights were removed and all retired out of sight

156

and the calm sleep, so much desired, came and the breathing stopped without a sigh or struggle while yet it lasted. . . . I thought Your Majesty would sanction my asking to be allowed to see once more that dearly beloved Face and as I knelt by the bedside, I felt as if the ardent longing within me to convey some of the sense of peace and rest and heavenliness to Your Majesty would enable me to do it. O, how I missed the light of the beautiful eyes and the smile of recognition and life. How I felt for the poor poor children, coming to find these gone. . . . Nothing can exceed the friendliness of the Empress about every detail.'

Lady Augusta wrote to her sister the same day:

'We were aroused by a telegram from the Queen, telling of her anxiety and urging us to go direct to Baden. . . . She took a great deal of Chlorale at one time and lately had morphine punctures. The Empress blames the Doctor for having had resource to this so much as destroying her appetite. But in such a case, surely ease is the first and last condition. . . . Poor Pss. Ada [her daughter and niece of the Queen] learnt at Frankfort yesterday that all was over and the two sons, one in Tyrol and the other, Prince Hermann, on his way. . . . Dr. F. (the Empress's doctor) has just been here. He told me that the case was this. The local affection lost its activity and threw itself first, a few weeks ago, on the brain and then, at the end, on the lungs. He had foreseen cancer for years. All her symptoms pointed to it. . . . The Empress spoke her sympathy and asked what she could do and she said "Get my children, my dear dear children – poor Ada."

' "And your sister?"

' "Oh yes, my dear sister, my poor Victoria."

'. . . I wrote to the Empress and this morning She sent to me to go with her for her *last visit.* I felt much for Her. She loved her so tenderly and of course found in Her such a friend in heart and mind as she will not find again.

'. . . Max [Müller] Geoff. and we went to the Empress [after dinner]. She had told me we two ladies were to listen and the men to talk and we were to do needlework. At this She noticed that my countenance fell and quick as thought, she added "perhaps you have none, I will give you some of mine to do." So it was, and very pleasant. We remained till 11, talking on all subjects. She certainly manages admirably such things and O, how one wishes that the Queen had such opportunities of hearing interesting talk.

'. . . They spoke about Henry V, and the Empress was much amused by Arthur's conviction that he could make him see it to be his duty to abdicate, if he could only speak to Him.

'A. cross questioned me about the work and said musingly this morning, "I am afraid that unless the next person thoroughly understands the principle on which my Dear one worked at that *carpet*!! it will all come to a sort of mingle mangle!!!"

'In the afternoon, we walked and met Lord Torrington, the Manchester Couple and a number of other rather unattractive ones.'

On September the 24th, Lady Augusta wrote to the Queen:

'I have had the honor of receiving your Majesty's two telegrams of today. Your Majesty's intentions with

regard to the souvenirs to be placed by the beloved
Princess will be carried out and the Dean hopes to be
able to prepare such a short notice as Your Majesty suggests together with the account of the real ceremony at
which we hope to be allowed to be present. . . .

'The Empress sent for me this morning at 10 to accompany Her Majesty on Her last visit to the dear House.
On arriving H.M. found Prince Hermann at the door,
he having reached Baden shortly before. He was much
moved and affected, but in the midst of his grief he said
he would rather suffer thus than have known his beloved
mother suffering, as he feared sometimes when he saw
her in the summer, that she might continue to do. . . .

'The beloved Princess we saw once more as She lay in
Her lovely white muslin gown and spotless cap – a transparent lace veil (it looked to me like a shawl I had seen
Her or the beloved Duchess wear) over Her face. Most
beautiful she looked and more like Her dear dear Self.
But still there was something about the unclosed mouth,
as is so often the case, that altered the expression that
made me less grieve that Your Majesty should not have
been kneeling where I knelt, than I should have grieved.

'The Empress felt it much and spoke very sadly of the
terrible loss. . . .

'The precious remains had been taken to the room on
the ground floor which was filled with flowers – a cross
on the wall at the head and wreath and pyramids of leaves
and flowers everywhere. And even more heavenly than
before did Her sleeping face look. It soothed dear Princess
Ada and the altered expression of the mouth did not jar
upon Her I am thankful to say. She did not mention it.
Prince Hermann had. They allowed me to remain alone

and I kissed the beloved forehead and the lovely marble hand for Your Majesty – that wonderful hand which I always see before me.

'Prince Hermann was to place beside his beloved mother all that Your Majesty indicated.

'We dined quite alone with the Empress who spoke much and wished me to say that Her Majesty felt a good deal exhausted and would leave it to me to mention all that had taken place today, hoping to write Herself soon.

'We are deeply touched by the noble, manly, while tender and almost childlike grief and reverence of Prince Hermann. . . .'

Lady Augusta represented the Queen at Princess Hohenlohe's funeral.

'No friend, not even the Duchess of Hamilton was asked. I had a most unpleasant business in helping Prince Hermann to get rid of Ly. A. Loftus who had come with Lady Torrington. . . . I went up at one with 4 beautiful wreaths from the Queen and Princesses. . . . A most touching letter from the Queen: it is indeed really the greatest loss almost that she could sustain.'

The letters written by Lady Augusta when she returned to England are marked *private*, and respect for this fact prevents a full description of the grief of the Queen who suffered a reaction of the loneliness which was her obsession since the death of the Prince Consort. Lady Augusta went to Windsor Castle when she returned and found the Queen in despair over the fact that her daughters were married and filled with their own interests, from which she was excluded. The Queen's one comfort was Princess Beatrice, 'and I'll take care that She never marries. . . . She is quite happy at home and contented and sweet tempered . . . and without jealousy.'

'I said she had no one to be jealous of.'

The Queen had decided 'that no married daughter is of any use.' Lady Augusta adds, 'She is so innocent and lovable with it all.'

CHAPTER IX

Princess Alice and Strauss. Prince Leopold at Oxford. The Empress of the French visits the Queen. An honour for Tennyson. Lord John Russell's book. Lord and Lady Salisbury. Carlyle and Froude in the Park. Charles Kingsley at Westminster. Death of John Stuart Mill.

CHAPTER IX

1872–3.

Lady Augusta and the Dean went to Windsor again in December, when she found

'Mary Ponsonby in great disgrace, having never visited the cottagers at Abergeldie and only been once to Church.' The Queen 'had a very interesting and nice religious talk with A. – like in the early days of Her Widowhood, and has since begged him to write it down for Her to refer to.'

Back at Westminster, Lady Augusta went

'to [Baroness Burdett] Coutts to a committee about the slave trade, where Samuel [Wilberforce] of Winchester presided – asleep most of the time, as Kath. maintained.'

Next day, to dinner 'with Mr. Holman Hunt, just returned from the East,' and one evening she

'dined with the dear Hatherleys.[1] He had a letter from a friend in India who had been with Lord Northbrook [Viceroy] on his tour – the Rajahs vied with one another in the magnificence of his reception – but the one who

---

[1] Lord Hatherley, Lord Chancellor. He was a deeply religious man, and even as Lord Chancellor he continued to teach at a Sunday School in Westminster, as he had done when he began his career as an unknown young barrister.

succeeded in carrying off the palm, was one who had dressed his bodyguard of 30 black men, in Highland costume, with flesh coloured leggings!! thinking by the pictures that that was the correct thing.'

December 10.

'. . . On Friday I went with Miss Merryweather, the most intelligent Lady Superintendent of the Liverpool Nursing School, to see the Hospital in Gray's Inn Road, nursed by Secular nurses, trained by one of her pupils and under a committee of which Lady Grant was a principal promoter. It was very satisfactory. Mr. Conway wishes to have them here [in Westminster]. Others would like Miss M. to start one with us, which would in some ways perhaps be better – but either would be welcome. From Miss M.'s experience, I should like to have female resident physicians. It is very difficult to keep all straight between the young doctors and the nurses, and even when they are Sisterhoods, there are nurses exposed to the same dangers.'

On December 14th, Lady Augusta went to Windsor to dinner,

'very pleasant indeed. Prince of Wales specially agreeable and the others and all were cheery and nice. Pss. of Wales spoke to A. about Strauss [1] and how sad it was that Princess Alice should see so much of him and accept the dedication of a book of his. A. agreed, but tried to excuse Her on the ground of his being one of the few very intellectual persons at Darmstadt, and thus attracting Her, but he was quite pleased with the Pss. of Wales' interest and

[1] The German critic who lived in Darmstadt and who knew Princess Alice, now Princess of Hesse.

166

Her more serious comments. She told him she had read the report of his lecture on Socrates, and supposed the account of the wife had been taken from *me*!!

'Prince Leopold delighted with Oxford. . . . He has only a few select undergraduates to associate with, but almost every evening, three or four of the Professors make most agreeable conversation at dinner. So good for him. . . . Did I tell you the state the Queen is in with Gladstone for pushing Ireland for the P. of W.? Of course there are great dangers for one like Him – but it is so difficult to find anything else and so bad for Him to idle. H.M.'s arguments and objections certainly have much weight – but the subject is a very anxious one.'

Early in the following year, their friend, J. A. Froude, the historian, returned from America

'pleased with the people but disgusted with the corruption of the Institutions and the low level of the highest cultivation – tho' the average is higher than with us. . . .'

January, 1873.

'H.M. has written me a most kind letter and sent me to read the most beautiful one, I ever ever saw, left by Queen Louise, with the Will, for the King Leopold [of Belgium]. You never read anything so touching and He must have had some wonderful qualities to inspire such love. I told you how amiable H.M. had been to A. Of the Prince of Wales she spoke favourably. . . .'

To Madame Mohl.

January 8.

We also have been reading Middlemarch [George Eliot] and admired its power greatly, but we thought the mistake

167

of the two marriages very painful, it haunted us like a
nightmare. . . . There is certainly no decrease of talent,
but the increase of painfulness, I think we may safely
attribute to the influence of the 'Spider,' as you call
him. . . . Arthur goes to Sandringham tomorrow, alone,
and he was at Windsor without me also, and was described
to me by an eye witness as wandering about the passages,
quite lost and *entirely out of time and space*!!

To The Queen.

Feb: 25.

Madam,

I am most deeply grateful for your Majesty's gracious
words and for having been allowed to read the enclosed affecting record of a visit [1] that must indeed have
left an impression such as Your Majesty describes. – I
wonder if the old Princess Murat is an American by birth.
– I think She must be the Member of the family who used
to attend the English Service in Paris, the Mother of the
Duchesse de Noailles? There is something so infinitely
sad in the thought of that little group, and as Your Majesty
says, the very cast of the Empress's countenance seems to
lend itself to heighten the tragic impression. . . .

The Dean is most grateful for the kind appreciation
of his little poem. I must own that I am quite incapable
of imagining when he does those little 'hors d'oeuvres' –
He seems to me to have been constantly busy with other
things, and suddenly he says, 'Oh! I have put those
thoughts together' – and proceeds to put them on paper –

He bids me say that it is evident on further inspection
of the Irish Bill, great difficulties present themselves,

[1] *Of the exiled Empress of the French.*

168

which will no doubt be fully discussed. – Your Majesty could not have given us so much pleasure by anything as by the Draft of that delightful letter to Tennyson,[1] which will cheer and warm his true and loyal heart – We dined with him at Mr. [Fred] Locker's last night – I had received the draft just before coming out and I could not help fancying all the time, what great pleasure was in store for him. –

Later.

The Dean thinks Lord [John] Russell's Book very interesting and touching as the work of so aged a States-man and as characterised by that youthful 'naivete' which Your Majesty remarks, and of which those Pages are so curious an example! –

He thinks it, as Your Majesty says, very ill written, filled with most careless repetitions and with a strange mixture of knowledge and ignorance – but still he feels that it contains in substance a real insight into the true nature of Christianity, and that it might have been, if it had been better arranged and executed, exceedingly useful. –

To Lady Frances Baillie.

March 5.

. . . Tomorrow we are to take Tennyson to Windsor, to meet H.M. at Frogmore, to see the Mausoleum.

. . . Hatfield is pleasant and they [Lord and Lady] Salisbury are nice with their children. They tell the eldest [the present Lord Salisbury] (he is ill), all about affairs,

---

[1] The Queen discussed Lord Tennyson's elevation to the Peerage with the Dean and was apparently advised by him in deciding the character of the Honour bestowed on the poet.

all that is done in the Estate, and explain that the others may choose their professions, but his is fixed for him and he will have to work the hardest of all. He is very dear and very fond of his parents. . . . Lady S. is mad with Eton, for she says, in public examinations, the Eton boys are nowhere and that you cannot get them prepared for such an examination there. . . . Lady Salisbury told me all her plans about her boys, and then she said 'I dare say it will all turn out as ill as the rest – but still one can but try, tho' it is discouraging when one knows it is for Turf Clubs.' . . .

. . . Gladstone consulted some stupid obscure men about his Irish Bill, who misled him. . . . Poor Canning made a slip, I understand, for he sanctioned the scheme at first and then found the Irish prelates opposed. He was rather in a fix. He dined at the Metaphysical yesterday and Arthur said that his pretentious talking, to conceal his meaning (if he had any) quite made him (A.) sea sick.

None of her contemporaries did more to arouse the Queen's interest in the personal lives of Her subjects than Lady Augusta, whose letters made the Queen aware of people and circumstances which would never have come Her way. This fact is proved in such letters as this, which records Lady Augusta's meeting with Carlyle,

'walking in the Park yesterday and got out of the carriage to walk with him. He was very charming and full of life and wit, but suddenly he changed his tone and told us with what profound interest and emotion he had read "Memorials of a quiet life" [by Augustus Hare] which he had come across by accident, how it had impressed him

as few things had done and how the simple record of the
life and labours of Mr. and Mrs. A. Hare in the little
parish of Alton had been to him the most affecting of
histories and better than all the apologies and defences of
the Church of England, and that he could not believe that
an Institution that could shew many such humble centres
of piety and cultivation, refinement and charity, had not
power in it still!

'It was very affecting to hear him speak – One could
hardly have believed that the worshipper of "force," as he
is supposed to be, would have been attracted by so simple
a record as this, the power of which, was the power of the
indwelling spirit of love and holiness.'

To Lady Frances Baillie.

Ap. 2.

I told you did I not that we met Froude and Carlyle
in the Park the other day and got out and walked with
them. C. is full of Froude's Irish Book and very mad at
the prospects of Europe threatened on all sides by the
wave of lying superstition and nobody seeming to heed it
or to have Cromwell's wisdom and energy – Only perhaps *Proossia* sees and acts. –

A few weeks later Lady Augusta wrote to the Queen:

'Dear old Madam de Bunsen is much interested and
gratified by the publication, unknown to her beforehand,
of her husband's correspondence with the late King of
Prussia. She had not the permission to quote from this
correspondence in "The Life" but it is very interesting
and throws much light on her work. – The letters are
published by the Queen Dowager and she has been
pleased to hear that the Emperor was specially anxious

171

that it should be done with every consideration for M. de Bunsen's family.'

To Lady Frances Baillie.

March 12.

. . . Young Prothero, of whom James [1] is so fond, the master at Eton, is a great reformer and is disgusted with the world in general, but Eton in particular and finds it so difficult to do anything, that he will not remain. He also says that it is all but impossible to be trained at Eton with a chance of taking a good place at a difficult examination. Marlboro' and Cheltenham he thinks far the best. . . .

March 28.

. . . H.M. was very dear on the 16th when I went down. I went quite late, in pouring rain. H.M. much occupied with the crisis. Gladstone's letters like volumes, and involved in the most wonderful way. . . . Prothero is indeed a new, impossible broom. I have no doubt but Mary Ponsonby explained that Hornby [2] is thought not to have the clear sightedness and decision required in a Headmaster – and that many are unhappy at the effect of this on the general discipline.

March 31.

. . . How pleased you will be to hear of the Kingsleys [3] here. People seem much pleased and when I heard him talking with Motley on Friday, I did feel it was a privilege to have such an intellect brought into this sphere . . . the Sacrist, Bacon, took Arthur apart to say that he was

[1] *Col. James Evan Bruce Baillie, of Dochfour, nephew of Lady Augusta.*
[2] *Headmaster of Eton.*
[3] *Charles Kingsley, the writer, appointed Canon of Westminster.*

indeed thankful for the appointment of a Broad Church-man – for knowing it was in Mr. Gladstone's gift, he had been afraid he might have appointed a Puseyite, and they were the most troublesome people that ever were in any Church!!

Do you see that the horrid Duke of Meiningen has married an actress. . . . How shocking!!

To the Queen.

May 10th.

The Dean is much shocked by the sudden death of John Stuart Mill. – We spent an evening in company with him on the Tuesday or Thursday after Easter and he pressed us to visit him at Avignon! Mrs. Grote's descrip-tion of his distinguished Father, shews how much more *lovable* a person was the Son – and unsatisfactory as many of his opinions were, the Dean always valued his influence much, on account of his independence of party.

. . . The black singers came to visit the Abbey yester-day and I undertook to lionize them in part – Your Majesty would have been amused to see an army of note books produced – greatly to my alarm, for I felt very shy when I found all my commonplace remarks taken down!! they are most intelligent and bright, poor things. – After we had left, they sang one of their Hymns in the Abbey and most beautiful it was –. . .

I can not resist enclosing a note just received from Miss Thackeray in which she speaks of an evening at Farringford with the Tennysons. She herself is delightful.

Lady Augusta and the Dean apparently went to France and Switzerland in May. But there is only one letter recording the visit and it was written to the Queen.

'We made out our little tour very successfully. – One of the two evenings we spent in Paris on our way – we were at Mme. de Mussey's where we saw the Duc and Duchesse de Chartres and the Duc and Duchesse d'Alençon. The Duc de Chartres I would hardly have recognised; – he looks well and handsome, but more matured tho' he still has his pleasant bright young expression – The Duchess has even improved in looks. – I was much interested in seeing the Duchesse d'Alençon – People admire Her, but I think one must be near to appreciate Her beauty of expression. – There was such a formidable circle round the Princesses that neither Mme. Mohl nor I had courage to break thro' it to do more than make our devoirs on arriving – The Princes I had an opportunity of talking to and they were most friendly and pleasant. – The Duc d'Alençon was charming – it reminded me of old Frogmore days and His beautiful Mother, and the dear Duchess's interest in the Sons, and made my heart feel very full. –

'I ascertained that the Duc d'Aumale had sent his Speech at the "Institut" to Your Majesty. – All who heard it spoke most enthusiastically both of the matter and the manner. –

'We slept at Troyes on our way to Geneva and were delighted with the old Town, where our Henry V was "fiancéd" in one church and married in the other. – At Basle we were disagreeably surprised by finding snow on the ground, and the journey from thence, over the high table land by Berne was colder than I can describe. – When however we came thro' the long tunnel and saw the lovely blue lake of Geneva below us, with the blue of Heaven reflected in its dear waters – we forgot all the wintry approaches, and tho' the North wind continued to blow sharply, it was only reviving – I thought how much Your Majesty would have enjoyed it and was constantly wishing for Your Majesty and recalling all the expressions of admiration and delight which the Lake and the Mountains called forth in those precious letters. – '

In June of 1873, the Shah of Persia came to England and although he later amused Aldershot by appearing on a horse with a tail dyed pink, and who was said to have slaughtered a sheep as a sacrifice on the floor of his room at Buckingham Palace, his arrival was a splendid occasion and on that day, when the Queen appeared, Lady Augusta wrote to her:

'My heart was *so full* on seeing Your Majesty today that I felt impelled to venture to send it,[1] though we have it only in this untidy form extracted from the Magazine. –

'I trust that Your Majesty will not have been too tired and was repaid by the beauty and interest of the scene. – Like the Arabian Nights indeed. . . . Certain it is, that Your Majesty's Subjects have not for long had so much enjoyment – the Streets have been quite a sight – and as Your Majesty has heard, all the way to Greenwich and wherever there has been standing or sitting room along the routes. –

'Does Your Majesty know one of the Shah's titles "Asylum of the Universe"!!

'I conversed with a very ragged man in Westminster, who had seen him arrive and was indignant with the stories circulated. "I expected to see a *Savage* and he is a very pleasant looking Gentleman"!!!!

[1] *A newspaper cutting.*

'I enjoyed much watching His enjoyment of the Reel at Buckingham Palace. . . .'

To Madame Mohl.

August.

We spent two days very pleasantly in the I. of Wight last week – one at Osborne and one at Carisbrooke. The Queen was very charming and the Crown Prince and Princess of Prussia captivated us more than ever. He was full of his visit to Munich and much impressed by his reception there – it is delightful to hear him speak of such subjects. There is such heart and such modesty in all he says and feels.

The Vicarage of Carisbrooke looks up to the beautiful old castle where Charles I. was prisoner, and from it – the Castle – you look over the whole island. A. preached a charming sermon, introducing the whole history of the place in the way you know.

In August, Lady Augusta went to Broomhall, Dunfermline, and from there continued her letters to the Queen. Just as she was consulted on a variety of questions as of old, so did the Dean continue as theological adviser to the Queen, and Lady Augusta's papers include an interesting letter which he wrote to H.M. about this time. His letter was no doubt in answer to the Queen's interest and concern over the religious difference of Pr. Alfred and his proposed Russian bride, who belonged to the Greek Church.

Aug. 20/73.

The Dean has read with much interest Your Majesty's correspondence. . . . He quite agrees with the Queen

176

that the danger and difficulty of dealing with the Roman Catholic Church extends beyond the political inconveniences –. There are, it seems to him, two kinds of difficulty – One arises from the superstitions or erroneous views held by Roman Catholics. These are, no doubt, held by the Greek Church and, in different forms, but often with the same results, in many of the Protestant Churches –. Some of the ceremonies and tenets of the Lutheran Churches are astonishingly more like the Roman Catholic, than any of those in the Church of England; and it has been pointed out by G. Hallam and Lord Macaulay how some of the most pointed errors of the Roman Catholic Church are found in the tendencies which produced the Free Church in Scotland. – These difficulties will always come forth, not only in the State, but in families. But the Dean thinks that they may be overcome by [indecipherable] firm conviction of the larger, grander truths of Christianity, with the understanding of the circumstances out of which these errors, in their various forms, have arisen.

There is, however, in the Roman Catholic Church, the peculiar evil, beyond these errors –: that it is like an aggressive party, with a party organisation, always trying to gain converts and acknowledging no laws and no religion, but its own. – From this evil the Greek Church, and most Protestant Churches are free –; and it is (the Dean wd. suppose) on this distinction that the Crown Princess wished to lay stress, in speaking of the contrast between a marriage with a Greek and a marriage with a Roman Catholic –. It is, at any rate, a distinction from which he trusts that Your Majesty may derive consolation, in the midst of the discomfort that may arise from the introduction of an element so foreign to English and Protestant feelings, as the Russian marriage may invoke. –

Lady Augusta to the Queen.

Broomhall, Aug. 29.

Lady Ruthven, who is as active and lively as ever, is full of the same interest tho' her deafness, which she bears most beautifully, cuts her off from much enjoyment. – She is greatly beloved and has been elected to preside the School Board of the District!! She built some years ago, among her good deeds, a very nice school in the Village on the 'façade' of which is a medallion of Your Majesty with the inscription 'God bless our beloved Queen Victoria' – On Tuesday afternoon we came by the Boat from Leith to our own Pier, a most lovely sail on a most lovely afternoon. On board we met several coming like ourselves from a distance for the 'celebration,' and to my great delight I was recognised by several as belonging to the 'Familie of Broomhall' which is the thing that pleases me most, as it does to see 'Dean Stanley' counted among them. –

To the Queen.

September 6.

At Broomhall, we were looking over, with a view to Lady R. Weigall's Memoirs, some letters addressed to my Grandmother, Lady Elgin by the Queen, then Duchess of Wurtemburg, between the years 1795 and 1803 – and it touched me much to read such kind and afft. words from Your Majesty's Aunt, to one to whom her family all owe much, so long ago! There were allusions in the letters to my Aunt, Lady Charlotte, which made me think that She

178

must have had some of my own beloved Sister's wit and spirits. –

We are very glad to learn that Your Majesty has met with some one so likely to suit at Crathie[1] and to be all that Your Majesty would desire, the connexion with dear Dr. MacLeod is a great recommendation, but it is not a choice that can be made in a hurry. –

To the Queen.

Sepr. 14.

We have much enjoyed the Sermons of our new Canon [Kingsley] today – Afterwards we paid some visits in certain Alms Houses in Lambeth belonging to Westminster, and were greatly interested in the conversation of an old Guardsman who served five years in the Peninsular War and was at Waterloo! – the latter he said was child's play compared with the Spanish Battles, especially the storming of San Sebastian which he described in the most graphic way, as well as the hardships of the whole campaign, food, clothing, lodging, pay – they were miserably off for everything – it makes one's blood boil to hear such a living comment on the all too well founded complaints of which the Duke of Wellington's Despatches are full – This fine old man is 85 – he has had five wounds and is a great sufferer, – but is full of intelligence and interest – His name is Murray and he enlisted at 15. being I suppose an Orphan, for he wound up, almost with tears in his eyes – 'I have always been among strangers but the goodness of God has been round me all my days. Oh! God has indeed been a Father to me' –

One saw that this was said in all simplicity and truth

1 *The church at Balmoral.*

179

and that it came from his heart, and the kind faithful
admiring way he spoke of the Niece who takes care of him
and of his neighbours gave evidence of his sincerity. – I
only venture to mention this because I think Your Majesty
will like to know that such a fine old Veteran survives. –'

To Lady Frances Baillie.

October 3rd.

. . . Today we had a nice adventure – I had always
wished to see after the poor old Lady of 82 whom I met
in the Abbey and who is so happy *on* her *Books* at 4/– a
week! I remembered the Street and No. but not her name,
and I found the Street was near the Waterloo Station –
However, when we got there, we asked and were told it
was at least 1½ mile further on, and *then* we must ask –
We trudged and trudged and asked, and at last reached
the spot. . . . We knocked at a humble door and out
came our dear old Lady but looking so ill! – She said it
was the decay of nature which she must expect and she
had besides, a good deal on her mind. – After some ques-
tioning she told us all her affairs and late history, and we
listened quite amazed at the choiceness and elegance of
her diction, in spite of an occasional *h* omitted or introduced. The upshot at which we arrived was, that a debt
of 30/6, incurred for the furniture of the poor room, and
for which *cruel* interest was exacted by a neighbouring
tradesman, kept her almost at starving point and pre-
vented her knowing an easy moment or living in the
comfort! she might, on her £20 pension, as the widow of
an East India Coy.'s Servant. I fumbled in my pocket
and found I had exactly that sum, and after a few more
enquiries we told her we would pay her debt. – She

jumped up, 'would not we like to see her do it? She would come with us,' and off we started – She had said little – but when half way, she turned round, trembling from head to foot, and looking in my eyes, she almost sobbed out 'O and am *I* to be a free woman again' and seized my hand. – The vile usurer was out, and a smart, flaunting girl alone in the shop, so she could not pay, but she was to return at early dawn tomorrow and she again seized our hands and said 'if God spares me till the day before Xmas, on that day I shall kneel in yr. Church to give Him thanks – and you shall see me at yr. door – I can not go so far except just on the days I go for my Pension, and the day before Xmas is the day' –

She had told us how many weeks that was, for she had been counting and counting, to see how she could eke out her poor little means over those weary months. We told her all we wished was that she should have an easy mind, and be enabled to read her Books, in peace and comfort! –

Dean Stanley to the Queen.

Rome, Oct. 12.

. . . At Rome the Dean found Sir Henry Holland, who in his 85th year was going on to Naples, which he had not seen since 1816, when he was there with Queen Caroline. Sir H. H. had a private interview with the Pope, who was much amused at finding someone older than himself. Sir Henry thought that, unless by some external cause, the Pope had four or five years more life yet. There was also Barthelemy St. Hilaire the intimate friend . . . of M. Thiers, who at the age of 68 had come to Rome for the first time, after also visiting Constantinople and Atlas – quite with the enthusiasm of a boy. – and full of interesting remarks on the state of France. – Your Majesty may have heard us speak of the blind old Duke of Sermonetta – far the most interesting of the Roman Nobles. He gives an excellent account of the present state of Rome in two words – in saying that it is like a '*moulting cockatoo*,' the old feathers gone, and the new feathers not yet come. Another person that we have met is the great Bavarian General of the War of 1870, Von der Tann – He is a powerfully gracious and accomplished old man – and was very much gratified on hearing from the Dean that even some of the French that he had met, spoke of his kindness –. 'Generally,' he said, 'they tell everyone that I was an ogre who ate little children.'

The Dean heard of a legend at the Certosa of Pavia – a magnificent Carthusian Monastery that he went to see. It was, that many years ago, two children of a king of England came to Italy – and when they returned, the king asked them whether they had seen the Certosa of Pavia. They answered that they had not – and the King of England immediately sent them back all the way to see it. This story, the Dean thought, would amuse Your Majesty.

Lady Augusta to the Queen.

Nov. 13.

We resolved to carry out our original plan and to halt at Moulins where we wished to see some antiquities. – The Bishop, to whom we had a letter, asked us to stay with him, and in him we found a Member of one of the oldest and best families of France, nearly related to Count Mensdorff and a staunch legitimist – After witnessing the hopes of all his 'entourage,' it was dreadful to arrive

in Paris on the very day of the publication of the unfortunate letter!! The Legitimists of the Provinces however
recovered it more easily, they only think that that for
which they have waited so long, is postponed yet a while,
to triumph in yet more unsullied *whiteness*; but the Mon-
archial party in Paris and at Versailles were less easily
consoled, and it was very difficult to escape from the
alternatives of incurable stupidity, or worse still, something like a breach of faith attributable to a want of
resolution and courage at the critical moment. – I *hope*
it was not *that* in the 'petit fils de Henry IV'! but it is
cruel to the Orleans family and their honor has been put
to a severe test and has stood it, that is a comfort whatever
happens. – Some one said to the Duc de Broglie as a
solution of the difficulty 'il y a le cholera à Vienne, il
pourrait gagner Frohsdorf'? –

'La Providence n'a point de ces *complaisances*-là pour la
France' was the reply – We attended the Bazaine trial
twice, and were in the greatest admiration of the dignity
and power and ability of the Duc d'Aumale – People in
France are lost in astonishment and there is but one
opinion on the subject. – His mastery of every detail of
this most difficult and complicated subject shews a power
of intellect and an industry of no common order – I kept
thinking how proud the good Queen and his beloved
Sister Queen Louise would have been of him. – We
called on the Duc de Nemours and were able to speak of
this, but alas! politics were too painful to be alluded to.
We dined with the Duc de Broglie the day before we left –
the difficulties and disappointments were almost overwhelming but he did not seem to lose heart or courage,
though he said he still looked back with the greatest

pleasure to his stay in England and never regretted anything so much as having to leave his post there, just when he was beginning to know and understand English Society. – Dear Mm. de Ste. Aulaire is pleased to think that her *step grandson* is to have the honor of representing France at Your Majesty's Court. . . .

I hope that Your Majesty may have seen the extract from the 'Nord' announcing that the *Archbishop* of Westminster and his *Wife* were to go to Russia [1] – he to perform the English ceremony!

If people will take names that do not belong to them, dreadful aspersions on their characters are liable to result from it.

Lady Augusta to the Queen.

Dec. 21.

Madam,

I trust that Your Majesty made a comfortable journey and had a good passage – I saw dear Princess Alice on Friday night, looking very pale and tired –

. . . The Dean was much interested and gratified by his interview with the Duke of Edinburgh on Wednesday, and felt more at his ease and more able to speak with His Royal Highness than he had ever done before – I feel I may venture to express this to Your Majesty, for Your Majesty well knows that is not personal pleasure alone – but the thought that in every such indication there is an additional hope for such a future as we hope and earnestly pray for. –

[1] *For the wedding of the Duke of Edinburgh and Princess Marie of Russia.*

CHAPTER X

To Russia for the marriage of the Duke of Edinburgh and Princess Marie. Prince of Wales and
observance of Sunday. Lady Augusta and the
Dean guests of the Crown Prince and Crown
Princess of Prussia, on the way. The Crown Prince,
the Emperor, Bismarck, and the Dean.

H.I.H. PRINCESS MARIE, AFTERWARDS DUCHESS OF
EDINBURGH

CHAPTER X

1873–4.

By August of 1873 the Queen was full of the coming
marriage of the Duke of Edinburgh to Princess Marie,
the daughter of the Czar of Russia.[1] The Prince and
Princess of Wales and Prince Arthur were to go with the
Duke to Petersburg for the ceremony. On August 8th,
the Queen wrote to Lady Augusta:

'I shall see you tomorrow, I wish to prepare you for
what not only I, but Alfred and others (including the
Dean of Windsor and Lord Granville) are very anxious
for. It is, that I am very desirous that your Dean should
perform the English ceremony at St. Petersburg, and
that you should attend as one of my ladies. You travel

[1] The marriage of the Duke of Edinburgh to the Russian Princess
had been anticipated for some time, and in May of 1871, Lord Granville had written to the Queen that he thought 'the Russian Princess
would be a more desirable marriage for the Duke of Edinburgh than
an English subject, a Catholic Princess or a daughter of the King of
Hanover.' But he wished to discuss the matter with Mr. Gladstone,
'who is very anti-Russian.' The Duke of Edinburgh was heir to the
Duchy of Saxe-Coburg, and in May of 1871, the Queen had talked to
him about his future plans, 'found him very sensible, being quite
willing to go to Germany, and take more part in the affairs of
Coburg, if his uncle would let him, and spending part of the year
there.' The Duke of Edinburgh and Princess Marie became Duke and
Duchess of Coburg.

so much, and dread cold so little, that, as in January the Russian climate is said to be healthy, I hope you may be able to undertake a mission which will require great discretion, and which will be a comfort to me. But you must fully consider whether you can manage it, and that is why I have thought it best to write before I see you both.'

Lady Augusta to the Queen.

Nov. 27/73.

Your Majesty knows that there is nothing I would not try and wish to do to be of any use and comfort, and that the future happiness and welfare of the Duke of Edinburgh and this dear young Princess, and these as affecting so nearly Your Majesty's happiness, are nearer my heart than I can possibly describe. It will be a deep source of thankfulness to me if I can be of any use or comfort at so anxious a time owing to the entire oneness of thought and feeling and life that has existed between my sister and myself since she could speak! – I always think that I know what it is to give up a daughter from what I went thro' when Fanny married!!

Our plans are in abeyance till we receive orders from Your Majesty – we are told that there is a very remarkable and interesting festival on the Neva on the 18th (Russian twelfth night), if it happened that we were arrived by that time, it would interest the Dean much to witness it.

In the more humble sphere of dress I require some instructions. When I read the Empress' affecting words and think of this terrible separation, with my whole heart I give thanks in the knowledge of the loving tenderness which Your Majesty will ever shew to this new Daughter and I rejoice to see in the tone of the Empress' letter a proof of the confidence Her Majesty seems already to feel in the Maternal affection which Her precious treasure will find and to which She commits her.

Jan. 3. 1874.

Your Majesty may rest assured that no human creature shall suspect the motive of our interest in the young Princess of Mecklenburg – We have the most natural reasons for being interested in the Princess and her Mother – The Grand Duchess Helen was the play-fellow of my dear Brother Elgin when they were children, and was most kind to us both when we met H.R.H. at Lucerne some years since. – The Dean has now been study-ing the Russian Services in translations, given by H.I.H.

We have been accumulating warm things and hope to be quite prudent and to do as the Russians do. – I really dread the hot rooms almost as much as the great cold.

January 7.

. . . I trust that Your Majesty was agreeably impressed by the Duc de Bisaccia, I am so pleased to think of a representation of that 'old France' having been at Osborne and especially such a one. –

We heard yesterday that the Emperor is graciously pleased to lodge the Suite in the Palace at Berlin and are most grateful to be included – it makes a great difference at all times, but most so at this season when Hotels are so chilly and stuffy – Trusting to be able to send Your Majesty only pleasant telegrams and accounts. . . .

I will most fully avail myself of Your Majesty's gracious permission to ask any confidential questions that may arise for solution, and with most respectful and affec-tionate wishes. . . .

It was arranged that the Prince and Princess of Wales and Prince Arthur, Duke of Connaught, should go to Russia for the wedding, and one of the problems faced before departure was the Russian observance of the Sabbath. In this connection, the Prince of Wales wrote to the Dean:

My dear Dean,

Many thanks for yr. kind letter wh. I received this morning. – I fully enter into all yr. views with regard to what you say concerning the observance of Sunday when we are at St. Petersburg, I am certainly very liberal on that subject myself – and think that in England and especially in Scotland – we are rather narrow minded and prejudiced as to the observance of the Sunday – at the same time I should be the last person to wish to shock my Countrymen by going to a Hall or Theatre on the Continent if I thought I should be doing so. Those I have never been to on a Sunday – As a rule I think 'do in Rome as the Romans do' although there certainly are limits. One certainly, as you know full well having travelled so much abroad, cannot spend Sunday exactly as we do here – and people would be both fastidious and absurd in expecting us to do so – but one can avoid doing many things which might give cause to adverse comment. As to travelling on Sunday abroad that is sometimes inevitable – and I think no one has any right to find fault with it – especially if one leaves England on a week day – and one's journey is prolonged on a Sunday abroad. – If one were to halt and lose perhaps 12 hours of one's journey because it was a Sunday – people would call one a humbug and very rightly so also –

I have written to you quite frankly and openly – as you

have done – and I really am much obliged to you for having written to me. We are now such old friends that I could never be offended by anything you write or say to me – and shall generally I have no doubt, agree with you.

Hoping that you and Lady Augusta have spent a merry Xmas and wishing you a very happy New Year, in which the Princess joins,

Believe me, My dear Dean,

Yrs. very sincerely,

ALBERT EDWARD.

Lady Augusta wrote to her sister, before they left for Russia:

'H.M. sent me a book of lovely Swiss views and a beautiful large jewel case – so convenient and acceptable for St. Petersburg. But on opening it, to A.'s rage, it contained six very lovely dessert spoons!'

In January they set out for Russia, staying in Berlin on the way. Crossing the Channel, Lady Augusta 'took some drops of chloroform, to the great contempt of the steward,' who told her that 'nothing keeps off sickness except staying on shore. . . . At Brussels Kennedy appeared with a bunch of white lilac.' They slept at Cologne. 'There was no snow on the ground, but all was frozen and the sun shone brightly.' And then to Berlin where they 'found Lord Odo Russell at the station.' They were driven in state to the Palace, where they were the guests of the Crown Prince and Princess.

'A whole suite of rooms, all warmed, and with blazing fires – real open fireplaces. They are the rooms which the First Napoleon occupied on his invasion of Berlin . . . all hung with family portraits, they are of old Hohenzollerns.

. . . The only want is wardrobes, of these there are none. While we were at dinner, in walked the Crown Princess, looking very well in Her strange court mourning. . . . The chapel is a tiny one and only held the family. The Boys so charming, much grown, full of interest and warmth – remembering all that had been said and done at our last meeting. . . . Princess Charlotte very good looking and almost friendly. Prince Waldemar and Princess V. nice. Princess Sophia very pale and the poor baby invisible. The Prince almost the same dear loved one. . . . Dressed to dine with the Crown Princess, a family dinner at 5 – all very nice. She talked long to A. after the Prince had retired. He has more than the usual business, the Dowager Queen having left him executor for all her papers. It was delightful to hear him speak of her – her kindness, justice, consideration. She retired after her Husband's death and gave up all – and yet she was so afft. and kind and full of sympathy that She remained the centre and bond of the family! loved the young couple much – and the Empress speaks just in the same way of Her – Lady E. and I sat apart while the Pss. and A. talked philosophy – politics etc., still hostile to the Present policy – I think he told her some truths on other subjects – useful I hope. – Very dear and nice of course – At 8.30 he and I went to the Empress who was most kind and pleasant –. . . The E. had been much more pleased with Pr. Alfred this time and seems hopeful. – We went on to tea at the Odo Russells where Lady Emma Osborne had preceded us. – Only the Legation – very pleasant – Ld. O. takes a gloomy view of the C. Prss. alienates him from the family – very unGerman – etc., etc., etc., he and I still hope that at any rate when she has the responsibility (long may it be before) she will be quite different – When she did the honors alone for the Shah she did – admirably. Very unhappy at not bng. asked to England – but She did not speak of that to us – O. is also very gloomy about the Bismarckean policy. I can not but hope he is wrong there also – "du reste" he is charming and she very agreeable. – They went this mng. at 7 to the station to receive the Wales party – who arrived quite untired!!'

Dean Stanley wrote:

'At 6 p.m. dinner at the Palace – exceedingly magnificent. The Emperor though recovering did not appear. But the Empress, the Crown Prince and Princess; Prince Charles (Emperor's brother), and his wife and son; Prince Frederick Charles, the great general and conqueror of Metz, and his daughter, Princess Marie (whom I took in to dinner); The Prince and Princess of Wales, Prince Arthur, and all their suite; the Odo Russells, Moltke, and Bismarck, were present. He (Bismarck) came among the last – a giant amongst them all in look and stature. He stalked across the room to Lord Odo and the Danish Minister, and begged to be introduced to me. I had but a few minutes' conversation with him, but enough to let me see his countenance, and hear his manner of speaking – much more gracious and familiar than I had expected, and exceedingly pleasant in his tone on the marriage. "It is very important that the two countries which *we* regard as friends to *us* should be friends to one another. War is a wild teacher, and anything which helps to keep him off is so much clear gain." I sat between the Crown Princess and Princess Marie – she is a very simple, innocent, pleasing girl.'

At the same dinner, Lady Augusta

'sat between Prince Frederick Charles and Moltke (with
whom I have old Balmoral souvenirs) and much enjoyed
my neighbours. Moltke is so modest, he will hardly speak
of "moi" – but he spoke of the agricultural question now
very burning in Germany. All the peasants migrate to
the towns having been too little paid for long, and there
are immense difficulties in consequence. . . . Prince F. C.
was very conversible. I did not think he was quite pleased
with the Court Martial and the French nation in regard
to poor Bazaine. I did not like to press him with questions
about what he could or could not have done, but I
believe the German officers are unanimous in thinking
that at any rate, after the first few days, he could not
have got out without sacrificing his whole army. Prss.
Charles, who was on the other side of her son, made him
present me and was very pleasant. She said "mon fils a
fait ce qu'il a cru être son devoir en venant rendre
témoinage à un ennemi injustement accusé." A. had a
little talk with Bismarck and liked him, at least found him
very frank and "avenant." He spoke very warmly of the
Russian marriage and said how important it was for
them that those whom it was the most necessary for them
to reckon as friends should be friends together. – The
Wales party looked most beaming and fresh – they go on
tomorrow night – The P. of W. was very nice to all –
spoke much to Bis. Bis. added to what I said above –
"War is a wild teacher and anything which can avert it is
a clear gain."

'Css. Hake came up to me and glancing at Lady E.
said "C'est Mme. votre fille"! We accepted gratefully

the arrangt .Princess Brandenburg asked much after you.
After dinner we went to the Bancrofts – he was at Moltke's
– she very charming. The Usedoms are here – we go to
the Museum with *him* tomorrow. Our apart. consists of
a dining room tendre en rouge foncé meublé en suite. A
reception room violet silk, id, id – a boudoir fawn colour
id. id. bedroom walls and all Pompadour cretonne –
smaller bedroom. A.'s dressing room blue satin – and
lovely boudoir beyond also blue satin – open fireplaces –
Lady E.'s on the same floor, bedroom and sitting room –
and a whole suite for servants behind. – Menials wait upon
our word or frown at every turn – the "Herr Bischoff" is
much admired, great efforts were made to locate him
in a different part of the Palace from the Hof Dame
which the Princess Royal with difficulty frustrated! A.
is *splendid* in a new fur coat and cap – All eyes will be
on the Bishop in St. P. – "*this* I have chosen as Gentlemanlike, serious, fit for a Bishop" – so we took it.'

At dinner, on the night before they left Berlin, Lady
Augusta sat next to

'a General, the tutor of Prince William. I complimented him on his pupil and the interest he takes in all
things. He said he only hears the topics of the day at his
Parents' table, but picks up everything and besides them,
his periodical examinations, which are those of other
German boys, he has passed with marked success. I spoke
of his great familiarity with all relating to the Ashantee
War. This, he said, was owing to M. Heckler's visit, he
having been in Ashantee as a missionary, had given them
a lecture on the subject when at Berlin, to the great
delight. After dinner at 10 the Empress came in to say

goodbye. The juveniles made a few faces over the dear Empress's manner. They had much better try to imitate her, in all else.

'The Empress very anxious – " Peace my dear Dean, you understand me. No exaggeration, no excitement." One could see that she is the depositary of many sorrows and perhaps resentments . . . at 2.45 we went to the Palace and saw the beloved Emperor. . . . He was "au civil" and apologised for his attire! Came to meet us and stood as erect as ever, but very thin and feeble on his legs. . . . The Empress was very glad we had seen him and could testify to his state. She took us upstairs and showed us her pretty rooms. – Then she sat and talked again of all the political anxieties and wishes, vaguely, but so as to make us understand in a general way. Very kindly and nicely as ever about the Queen and the marriage – pleased with it and with the Duke of Edinburgh. . . . She spoke very touchingly of the end of her own career and her anxieties being for her children and her country. . . . I think she is a most excellent and unselfish, unlittle woman.'

Bismarck spoke to Dean Stanley, and although the Dean

'could not find an opportunity of entering into ecclesiastical question . . . he talked in a perfectly easy manner on England, Shakespeare, etc., and in order to explain why he had not taken the Embassy in England, gave a most elaborate and accurate account of the inconveniences of the house in Carlton House Terrace. He gave us a cordial invitation to see him on our return and altogether left the impression of a much more amiable and gracious exterior and interior than I had been led to expect.'

CHAPTER XI

To St. Petersburg. Lady Augusta and the Empress.
The Dean and the Emperor. The Dean on the
Neva. Countess Tolstoy. Service in the Im-
perial Chapel. The Dean reads his sermon to
the Empress. Princess Marie. St. Petersburg
Society. The marriage. Lady Augusta dances
with the Emperor. The Emperor and his daughter.
His feeling for England. The richness of the
Court.

CHAPTER XI

1874.

From Berlin, Lady Augusta, the Dean, and Lady Emma
Osborne set out for St. Petersburg. Lady Emma did not
appreciate the heat of the train. She

'tossed and moaned and suddenly she exclaimed "Oh,
and to think that all this is to be done over again to get
home. If I can find a courier or anyone to marry me, I
shall settle at St. P. and never return." I can tell you
how we shouted and how great an occupation it was ever
after, to look out for the coming "man." '

Next day, when they reached the frontier 'a splendid
giant in uniform' and another arrived from St. Petersburg to attend them. The uniform and orders

'produced a great impression on us and Lady Emma
hesitated a good deal between them. . . .'

Lady Emma's suffering 'increased. She at last became
very sick.' The stationmaster recommended a medicine,
'which however, on smelling, poor E. declined. . . . Two
or three Doctors appeared at a station which we reached
in the early morning.' They had been summoned to
attend Lady Emma, but the servant

'on coming to the door and from the complete stillness,
concluded that we were all asleep, dismissed them and

probably saved her life. Think of three Russian country doctors!! She was so dear and nice all the time and so amusing and quaint that we kept laughing and crying at intervals at her misery. There were immense searchings of heart as to whether she should exert herself to make a toilette to impress "the uniformed attendant," or work upon his feelings by the sight of her squalid filth and misery. She decided in favour of the latter. . . . The landscape was flat and white. . . . At last the station was reached and there we found a carpet spread for our feet, a row of lovely Beings in uniform and white gloves on either side of it.'

The Dean described them as being 'dressed like the Doges of Venice in red embroidered cloaks and white ruffs.'

Lady Augusta continues:

'I saw that the moment was come for me to ape the manners of my betters and graciously and condescendingly, to bow from side to side in regal style – dazzling salons opened to receive us thro' which we only passed, however, into the Vestibule, where stood ranged, endless giant foot men in scarlet and gold great coats, lined with white fur – making the effect at the neck of white ruffs. I was bowed on – a delicious little Brougham opened before me, I stumbled into a pile of furs and before I recovered, was being whirled along the white streets as fast as two horses could carry me – Ly. E. and A. remained aghast and wondered why the two were to travel together, but one after another was captured and we all arrived separately at the door of the Palace where Pr.

The Dean on the Neva. wdc. 1874.

A SKETCH OF DEAN STANLEY ON THE NEVA

By the Hon. Sir William Colville

Galitzine, Vice Chamberlain, and another Vice received us in evg. dress and stars –

'Their apartment was magnificent. A drawing room "blue satin," bedroom "red satin," with satin curtains, half mast-high across, screening the beds . . . a beautiful bathroom with hot and cold laid on . . . one delightful Russian servant, so *very* respectable looking, waits on us chiefly and always conducts us about in the Palace – one footman speaking a little English and one, a little French, attend and go with the carriage, (they seem disappointed when we only have one carriage at a time) and a little English orphan girl, not knowing much English, waits on the rooms. Almost everything is new and smart, but whatever is not new, is *dusty*, and the suggestion of one of the ladies that we should have the carriage to drive to another part of the Palace, so as to avoid the passages on account of our gowns, though we have not adopted it, is not without sense!!! I cannot understand how it is so dirty.

'Ly. E. who is as sensitive as Mary Louise might be and suffers accordingly, declares that she has a Mujik in her apart. she first thought concealed as a spy, now she thinks a deceased one and that no efforts of hers to purify it are of any avail. Oh! the smells – natural and artificial – are past all belief – '

The Queen to Lady Augusta.

January, 1874.

I address this letter to St. Petersburgh, with two parcels, which require explanation, and which are entrusted to your special care. The one contains two sprigs of myrtle, which I ask you to put at once into a little warm water,

and to keep to the afternoon of the 22nd, to be placed in
the middle of a bouquet of white flowers, which I shall ask
you to order and give from me to Marie before the English
wedding, with this explanation, viz. that this myrtle comes
from a large healthy plant here which has grown from a
little bit of myrtle much smaller than these sprigs, which
was in the Princess Royal's nosegay, and which all the
brides (I think) have had a piece in succession. The
second box contains two Prayer-books: the one in white,
with an illumination of some verses, which I had painted
on purpose, is for the Grand Duchess; and the other plain
one is for Alfred – both to be given them on their wedding-
day and for the English wedding. My dear mother gave
my beloved husband and me Prayer-books, which I now
have, and often use, especially the dear Prince's.

Lady Augusta continued her narrative to her sister:

'We ordered tea and soup and then came a card from
Css. Bloudoff, an elderly Demoiselle d'honneur . . .
whom the Empress had entrusted with the care of us –
She soon appeared, looking like an old round French lady,
fat, with a cap – nice eyes, very clever – talking English
"a fond" and deeply versed in all theological and ecclesiastical questions. – She claimed an old acquaintance with
Arthur thro' his book . . . always goes into dinner and sits
next to him and, as the Empress warned me, tho' kind to
me reserves her greatest attentions for *him* – We have been
told that she is hated by a large section as a "devote" and
as exercising a considerable influence on the Empress and
making Her more Russian than the Russians, in her
religious zeal. This is very likely, but even tho' a zealot in
religious matters, she is very different from a Roman

zealot, and if her accounts are a little biassed by her zeal
and her pictures a little "couleur de rose," we saw others
and can check them by what we hear elsewhere – . . .
We all got ready *he* to be presented to the Emperor and
me to the Empress. Ly. E. wore a mauve gown so I put
on my green Paon. . . . In the agitation of the moment,
I searched for some of my diamonds, in the bags in which
C. Kanne had advised me to carry them, and two of my
most precious treasures were, I thought, missing!

'Imagine the state of mind in which I prepared to
approach the Imperial presence – and add to this that I
was told it was quite time and led to believe that a carriage
awaited me downstairs. Instead of which, it was one to
take A. to the Emperor. There was I planted, and unable
to recover Ly. E.!!! I ran up and down, calling to her
while my Russians looked on in mute amazement. – At
last we rejoined and we sped along miles of gallery, thro'
acres of Halls – past lines and lines of frowning old Czars –
thro' a little army of soldiers of all Regts. – with drawn
swords – and past fleets of Mujiks, sweeping and clean-
ing. – At last we reached the outer salon where were
five or six of the Ladies with whom we discoursed for a
few minutes and then were ushered in – The Empress was
quite alone, dressed in dark green with a sort of fluffy
trimming and black lace in her hair. She received us most
warmly and I was quite absorbed by Her grace and charm
and sweetness and pleasantness and by so much more of
looks than I expected. She is not the least like any of the
Hesse family, so much more distinguished and good
looking. – She spoke about us and our journey and A. etc.,
etc., and then the Gd. Duchess [the Bride] came, looking
most dear and bright. I did not think her perhaps quite

so pretty as her photo: but just as nice and frank as you described and so happy looking. The Duke came in and he also looked quite one of them and quite happy and at ease – There was nothing private – the Empress evidently did not trust Herself to talk much of what is nearest to Her heart and I believe has never allowed Herself to break down – Poor thing, I believe she is as much comforted and upheld as possible by the sight of Her Daughter's happiness, but it is simply *agony* to Her, – to them both.

'Today (Wedy.) – we saw the Emperor driving the Gd. Duchess in a traineau – only one servant – and on the last day at the Crimea, they had their last ride together.

'He broke down more than She with Arthur, and constantly has tears in his eyes. – They had one other Daughter older – who died at 7 and was so devoted to Him She used to entreat to be allowed to sit in his room even when He was busy, and would remain there hours, quite silent, if only she might see her Papa – Poor people, think of the agony of losing such a one? – They say that the Gd. Duchess has been a *friend* as well as a daughter – and that Her Mother quite leant on her for all sorts of decisions – She has a more abrupt manner than Her Mother – Tolstoy says She is very shy and that the effort to speak and be civil is still *very great*, and leaves something "a desirer" in her manner – but Her truth, frankness, simplicity, straightforwardness are something quite unusual and she is practical, sensible and without caprice. – She has been so very happy always that She has no misgivings. She is devoted to Him and has always been so tenderly loved that it seems quite natural that it should continue so. – She thinks herself quite determined to be a thorough

Englishwoman and her Mother's example in Russia has taught her how to adopt her Husband's country.'

While Lady Augusta went to the Empress, the Dean was ushered into the Emperor's room. The Emperor stood, quite alone, in full uniform, by a desk 'exceedingly gracious,' and the Dean said that he hoped the benedictions of both the Churches might descend on an event so happy for both countries. 'The only sufferers,' he added, 'are the parents.'

The Emperor's eyes filled with tears and he said, 'Yes, it is true, she has been the joy of our lives, but it must be.'

Lady Augusta's room in the Winter Palace looked down on the Neva.

'At every moment, under the windows, noiselessly in the slush, the little sledges fly past, some of the humblest nature, with peasant men and women in them. . . . Others with splendid steppers and trotters with chic looking harness and stylish drivers, a smart officer leaning back or a magnate in rich furs. . . . A few moments ago Uncle A. passed in a lovely sledge driven by a most picturesque coachman, drawn by two exquisite white horses – round and plump, but fleet of foot. . . . Behind the coachman sat a beautiful Archimandrite. . . . The Archimandrite . . . came in while we were at breakfast and, as bad luck would have it, I was in my dressing gown . . . considering how sumptuous I usually am, I was quite grieved to have made so poor an appearance. . . .

'To return, Pr. Bismarck seemed to me quite unobjectionable and his daughter has a very attractive, open, simple, almost handsome German face. He was very amiable and cheery and conversible – what a creature he is! They say here [St. Petersburg] that when he was Ambassador he got to talk Russian fluently, not the most refined, as he learnt it mostly Haroun Al Raschid-like, by going about among the peasants and common people, in the omnibuses and everywhere. . . .

'Tolstoy came with Miloutine, the demoiselle d'honneur – who wept a good deal over Ly. E. while Tolstoy rather pounded me. – At 4 we went to tea at our own Lady's, A. having in the interval gone round to write our names on the Royal and Imperial persons. We found A. at the end of our long walk writing his name on the last royal Book and he joined us.

'On Sunday we dressed in our best, She in green I in violet – (a splendid garment but rather more elaborate than I should have chosen myself perhaps) and A. in his Doctor's robes and sallied forth to the Imperial Chapel at 11 – I ought to have said that the night before on our way from dinner, we stopped to hear the Vespers at this same Chapel and were delighted with the music. Ly. E. and I were the only females, we stood just behind the altar rails within which the Emperor first and then all his Sons took their places. . . . The Chapel was filled with Officers all in the fullest dress uniforms and as we came thro' the Palace there seemed to be half an army standing about – We knew of the Emperor's approach by the distant sounds of the Band playing God save the Emperor – The Service lasted more than an hour, but the beauty of the music made it seem much shorter – the wonderful execution, the beauty of the composition and its originality – the magnificence of the voices – quite surpassed the Sistine Chapel music to my feeling –

'. . . A very delicious sight were the little Boys of the family all in uniform – a darling with a charming face and expressive – just like Augustus – They all filed out and we were fetched away by Chambelland and suddenly plunged into, *not* as I thought, a room full of diplomats and attendants, but of *Imperials* – First Pss. William (whom I took for her Lady) accosted me very amiably – then the Gd. Duchess, Marie Mihailovna and ainsi de suite – the latter stuck me before her in the one window where one could see the Emperor and all his family and suite, Ecclesiastical, and civil and Military, emerge from the Palace and cross the road bareheaded, to the little open temple created on the Neva – where the ceremony was to take place.

'She is a capital *fellow* that Gd. Duchess – most amusing and so handsome still. She said "me voici, mais j'en ai par dessus la tête voilà 54 ans que je ne manque pas une fois" and always comg. back on her 54 ans! – The Pss. of Wales and her sister were most nice and kind and cheery and when the Procession returned the Gd. Duchess – M. insisted on the Cesareona putting herself in front – "tu sais qu'il te cherche toujours des yeux, ton *Sach*," that is their name for Him. "Va, il sera triste s'il ne te voit pas."

'They seemed all very happy and comfy together. We could not hear the singing but the ceremony was very striking – The gorgeous group and then the old colours, taken in a hundred fights, carried by old soldiers and completing the picture.'

The Dean was also at the window, looking out at the ceremony on the frozen Neva. He wrote:

'Out of the Palace filed soldiers, chanters, Deacons, Archimandrites, Bishops, Metropolitans, the Emperor and all the Princes, bareheaded, to a small temporary Chapel on the frozen river, with a hole underneath it for the benediction of the water.'

Lady Augusta continued:

'The attitude of all was very reverent, and that of the people outside strikingly so – Thousands who usually stand round on the ice were collected on the right and left, in the mud, where they stood patiently till the gun from the fortress announced that the Cross had touched the water, then the whole mass raised their faces and crossed themselves. When all was over and the Princes came in, we all sat down at small round tables at Luncheon – I do not know how it was managed but in an instant all were seated in their right places. – The Grande Maîtresse was at ours and I saw an Officer come to speak to her, a quite unassuming man, and I stared at him as he spoke. Suddenly, she said "L'Empereur désire faire votre connaissance?" I was taken aback but he was so kind and civil, such a perfect gentleman, I was quite at ease in a moment – He advised me about Russian dishes! apologised for our rooms bg. low, hoped we had them warmed to our taste and told us how very much he rejoiced in the muggy weather we had, rather than in bitter cold!! The Empress did not appear – She had been so unwell and could hardly even find voice to speak to the few people she was obliged to see alone –'

On Monday morning, they went to the Museum in the Hermitage – 'a wonderful collection of Grecian antiquities,' particularly the 'Grecian sculptures of the habits of the Scythians 400 years B.C.' They were 'in magnificent rooms, rebuilt after the fire by the late Emperor, and ornamented with the most beautiful Russian marbles.'

'While we were there, A. was told that the Empress wished him to read his sermon to her at two. He had lent it and there was a hue and cry, but it was recovered in time and he went. She and the Grand Duchess were alone and it was most interesting, tho' the portions that referred to the parents almost upset him to read in Her presence. . . . While he was there, I went to [Countess] Tolstoy and sat out her other guests, and took her by storm. When I returned, I found A. entertaining a select circle in the bedroom!!! Why?'

Lady Augusta hurried into her 'nice yellow and brown gown, an agitating process,' and

'made a four mile journey to the other end of the Palace. I could have cried with fatigue. We were taken through the dining room and shewn our places. Mine was between the Cesarewitch and the Grand Duke Alexis, the sailor, and within two of the Emperor. . . . I did not feel shy and found my two Princes very pleasant – Alexis is a pickle, but intelligent, good looking and sensible. He talked like a book about schools, the training of girls, the drawbacks of institutes – also about National plays, and the theatre in general and the influence of good plays. The other cross questioned on agricultural and economical questions. He is rough but honest and good and kind – at one moment he was rather overdone with the Pss. of W. on one side and me on the other and exclaimed – "on me parle de tous les côtés, je ne sais plus ou j'en suis et voilà la Pss. de G. qui a oublié ce qu'elle voulait me dire!" – The Emperor made a little further apology about our staircase. The young people were opposite, looking very happy. He a little more shy – but she so natural and bright and smart – brimming over with happiness and admiration of him. She looked so very nice, with a white silk gown and a few red rose buds in her hair – People were smart and well dressed, but nothing extraordinary – The Empress looked very nice –'

Jan. 22.

Ly. E. and I ordered a Sledge and drove while he was away, to pay visits – the scene was delicious – the roads very rough – we shouted as the great bumps jolted us almost out of the sledge, but enjoyed the whole thing much and roared over one man who tho' he could communicate with us in French, conceived us to be perfect fools about our visits and set us quite at defiance – the names are so hopeless and confusing that we simply gave in and left as he directed –

We found Ly. Dunmore at home in her Cousin's beautiful Mansion. Decidedly mediocrity is not to be tolerated in Russia; one must be millionaire or nothing – any less makes life intolerable –

Tuesday we dined at 6 with Css. Bloudoff in her aparts. with Prs. Curanssoff and a few more, very pleasant – A young Pss. Troubetzkoy and her mother were there and a young Mme. Struve, and both were intelligent and told me much about their education and ways. Girls of all stations attend the same classes in the gymnase and young Troubetzkoy, after going thro' the course ending with a Cours de Pedagogue and getting her diploma, taught one of the most advanced classes of Russian History twice a week for two years – She was the Daughter of the Governor of the town – and I believe it is often done – In Petersburgh I imagined that the Parents seek for rather more select classes – but still the courses are very systematic and all go thro' examinations. They can hardly believe that only just lately has it been possible for women in England to obtain this test of their competency. – People spend all they can here to secure the best teaching for their daughters and do not generally expect them to give lessons only to superintend. I have no doubt that there is a tendency to cultivate 'a qui sont pour briller dans le monde' and that many if not most are very frivolous and superficial minded with it all – but they are wonderfully accomplished and well informed. M. de Grote the Marechal de la Cour who takes me into dinner and is very clever himself and a Courlandais or something says the women are much more cultivated than the men as in America. Properties are divided in the proportion of one 3rd for each son and one 7th for each Daughter – In speaking of the famine someone said that a great complaint is the ignorance of the Nobles of country matters and scientific matters applied to practical subjects – thus on their own estates and as Governors they neglect many of the most simple and the most essential precautions and improvements – We remained till 11 at the old Countess' on Tuesday afternoon Ly. E. and I went to an afternoon reception at Mm. Protassoff the Gd. Maîtresse – one of those quite like an old French lady. They all seem very civil but you know how stiff these things are unless one is intimate – and the smells! poor Emma goes into fits, for she suddenly discovers when some Princess is presented that She is no better in that respect than a Mujik and sometimes fears she may turn into one herself!

The Russians many of them – the pure type have it seems to me the vivacity of the French and the softness of the Italians – One immense fat old man we saw on his knees before a shrine pouring out his feelings in a gushing impetuous coaxing way most extraordinary to witness – rolling his eyes and gesticulating with his hands a sort of rubbing and twisting of them peculiar to Russians and Poles and as poor dear 'Hottock' used to do. – This man was in his enormous fur coat and as he rolled about from side to side looked quite like a bear. –

We almost always have a levée at Luncheon time and when any of our guests sit down I notice that Champagne is produced!! – The awful thing is that I know no one and not their names when they are gone! After tea at Bloudoff's at 4. E. and I went to call on a certain Nadine Bateneff, a maid of honor who is our delight. –

Her sister, much older was here. . . . Another one is more quiet and sedate – She told me that she had lost her heart to me and had asked Sir H. Elphinstone at dinner whether he thought I would be offended if she proposed to kiss me? How should Sir H. know I ask? – Ly. E. and I only wish we had more time to study all these peculiar characters –

When all was over and we came out after the signing of the Register as the Emperor left the room and bowed to all, Pillar elbowed herself out of the crowd, threw her arms round his neck and hugged him!

I told E., who was nearly fainting from exhaustion, that if anything could have revived her, the rage produced by this would –

'Yes!' she added, 'and the envy, for if I had only seen it in time I would have done the same'!!! On Wedy. we dined at the table du marechal. At these dinners one wears smart high dresses and I fall back chiefly on the Worth F. which is just the manner of thing they wear, chiefly in the day I wear with great effect my own 'gris deux tons' my brown velvet and my fawn silk, trimmed with velvet for smartest – my two mg. [dresses] I have as yet only worn for the Empress but they love one's old summer gowns, and so I give them – I dined here in my straw color brocade and brown velvet – (lovely) and have worn the 'old friend,' and my grey satin with black lace and cerise bows, with great effect at Adlerbey's Concert and the Gd. Duchess Marie's – Both times the D. of Coburg complimented me on my appearance and that I was always the same, which was nearer the truth than he imagined just then!!!

On Thursday mng. we went out to walk in the snow and I got so hot and tired in my big fur cloak that I had to come home in a cab (sledge). Poor Ly. E. could not make up her mind for fear of fleas! so she and A. walked and James and I drove in successive sledges. (They only hold one.) Of course the Driver had no conception of what we said till someone suggested 'Hermitage' and having got there I pointed the rest. –

Bloudoff had undertaken to order for me a bouquet H.M. wished me to give. All was arranged when suddenly she said coolly – 'no flowers can be had, they are all pre-ordered! –'

I was mad, ran right and left and finally Sir H. Elphinstone and A. started in a sleigh to ransack the town – They at last found one florist who had white roses

– and tried to make him understand – but in vain, quite in vain – till a happy thought struck him and he went to fetch a friend, a barber, who conducted the negotiation and one was promised for £7 and my peace of mind returned.

Bloudoff is much disliked by many as being too devote and influencing the Empress in that direction – but she is not fanatical in the way of intolerance – is very clever and very warm hearted – Tolstoy says she is the most beautiful combination of heart and head she ever met – the heart predominating and preserving all its youthful elan – She adores A. and always walks into dinner with him and talks all the time –

We came home, dressed in 'the old friend' and went to Prince Oldenburg's – a long Concert and very pleasant. The P. of W. very nice and sensible and looking so gentlemanlike and agreeable – They both please much here.

Winter Palace, Friday night, 10 p.m. Jany. 23.

By 11.30, or rather before, we were all dressed and our Maids had started with tickets for some of the numerous Galleries. . . . Lady Emma looked very nice indeed in a very delicate shade of pink, gown, train and feathers all alike and very pretty – Her 'Mama' [Lady Augusta] had a mauve satin gown and brocade train, both trimmed with velvet and lace and of the weight and length and heat of which she has nearly died this day – added to this, on her head and body, all the diamonds that she ventured to accept the loan of! (a great responsibility) – At 12 our most attentive dumb pilot set out with Lady Emma and me and we went thro' the long long corridors. We had been directed, or our guide had been directed to take us

DEAN STANLEY PERFORMING THE ENGLISH MARRIAGE CEREMONY
OF THE DUKE AND DUCHESS OF EDINBURGH IN ST. PETERSBURG

From a hitherto unpublished Drawing

to the 'Concert room' where the Grande Maîtresse and the Ladies on duty, with their beautiful costumes (white petticoats and red or green or blue velvet trains and bodies and hanging sleeves embroidered in gold) were assembled. Through this room passed all the Princely Guests, to a meeting room beyond and it was, I think, the Duke of Coburg, who looking out on the white landscape and leaden sky ventured to predict that the sun would come out – An arrangement was made by which a Gentleman was to fetch me from the Imperial Chapel in time to present the bouquet and Prayer Books from the Queen, when the Duke and the Grand Duchess entered it. – When once this was settled, I had not an instant's anxiety so perfect are the arrangements and the exactness with which all are carried out, down to the minutest detail – The hour we waited was a very solemn one, I felt what every second of it was to the Empress and to the Emperor whose pale face as He passed thro' and His struggle to look cheerful and to think of everybody were very affecting – It must have been one when the doors of the inner room opened and the Emperor and the Empress walked first thro' the long crowd to the Chapel, followed by the Grand Duchess looking very pale but sweet, and earnest and calmly happy. Six Gentlemen I think carried the long white cloth of silver train and the Mantle trimmed with ermine, and the Duke walked by her side, at least as they left the room, for I saw Her give Him her hand in a most touching and tender way.

The rather singular little high crown of diamonds, underneath which was a small bunch of orange flowers, would hardly have been becoming to one less young and bright looking but the Veil was very graceful and the whole effect truly regal. After the Bride came Czarevna and Her sister the Princess Royal, in blue and red velvet and gold, all three most becomingly dressed and glittering with diamonds and looking their very best. Afterwards came all the members of the Imperial Family and guests and then we. The Chapel seemed hopelessly full but still we were able to advance up to the rails and Lady E. and I stood just behind the Czarewitch and the Czarevna. . . . The music was more beautiful than can be told. . . . I thought the upward, confiding appealing look of the young Bride as Her eyes rested on the face of Her Husband while they walked three times round the Altar, was one of the most affecting and pathetic I ever saw –

The holding the crowns must have required a considerable effort on the part of the best men – but it was done with the utmost gravity and seriousness – . . . I waited about ten minutes in the Alexander Hall, reaching it thro' a dense crowd – then came the Emperor and Empress, both with faces betraying deep emotion and then the young bride and bridegroom – I gave the bouquet and the prayer books and they passed on to the altar table. . . . The Emperor greeted us as he passed out most kindly and with a choking voice said 'Je vous la recommande.' The poor Empress I cannot describe what her look was, 'éteinte' seems to me most to picture it. The bride was very sweet and gentle and quiet but cheerful and looked quite charming. We came home to our apartments at three thirty and had a cup of tea which we shared with Ladies of the Pss. of Wales. At four fifteen we returned along our long route and found the room crowded with ladies, the red velvet of the Maids of Honour seemed predominating. After a while we were taken into the immense hall where dinner was served. I do not know how many hundreds were seated, the Ladies and Gentlemen chiefly separated. I came next to the princes at one end and had an enchanting companion in the person of the second son of the Grand Duke Constantine, a very young sailor very clever and quite 'un homme du monde.' I suppose about fifteen or less and very good looking and most conversible. The dinner was beautifully served, the lighting of the room splendid. The plate and Sèvres china magnificent.

Patti, Albani and others sang delightfully and the room is perfect for music and alternately with the Italian there was some beautiful Russian music. The whole was over in an hour and then we were able at last to get to our rooms and take off our dreadful gowns and trains for an hour.

At eight thirty we returned for a third time. . . . I saw the Grand Duchess better and nearer, the small graceful head still so childlike, must have ached with the immense weight of jewels, the necklace of diamonds seemed to me the most beautiful I ever saw and the gown was studded with them, round the body and sleeves and down the front of the body and skirt. The Grand Duchess has a most lovely neck and shoulders. The Duke looked very happy and all were cheerful and looked well. The poor Empress did not appear.

I had the honor of going thro' the Polonaise with the Emperor. –

Winter Palace, Jan: 26.

We dined at 6 with the Emperor and Empress – the Crown Prince of Germany, Pr. Arthur, the two Gd. Dukes Vladimir and Alexis, Prince Alexr. of Hesse – the

D. of Coburg, Pr. Oldenburg – Ld. Sydney – Ct. Bruhl, Pr. Brandenburg, Cts. Tiesenhousen and Mme. Daria Trutchoff were the party. The Emperor took me in and Pr. Arthur sat on the other side. The Emperor spoke with delight of the impression made on him by his visit to the young couple at Tsarkoe Selo and the sight of their perfect happiness and comfort and satisfaction. – It did seem to drown nearly all selfish rights – if only she is happy!

I ventured to say that it would be different, but still this reflected happiness would be a very real happiness to them – 'Yes' he repeated 'reflected happiness – it will be that. – She is 20,' he went on to say 'and she has never caused us anything but joy. – We lost our eldest girl and we had so ardently wished for another – her birth was a joy and delight, not to be described, and her whole life has been a continuation. When she was in the school room, our hours did not suit and I could very seldom have her to walk with me, but then on Sundays She was mine and we always walked together – that was my fête – yesterday when the hour came round, I could not help telegraphing to her how I was thinking of Her and of our walks! –' (Is it not affecting poor man – his Wife is so delicate She can not take the place?)

He then told me of her excellent English nurse – She had taken care of all but the two eldest whom they have lost – their nurse, also English, died and this one came and She now lives in a nice house at Tsarkoe Selo – and was so overjoyed when she heard that her darling was to marry an English Prince!

. . . The Emperor spoke of his former visit to England in 1828 I think – he has not seen the Queen since H.M. wished him to take the Gd. Duchess over on a visit last year but he could not manage it. – He hopes now to look forward to a visit – Spoke of his Father's liking for England and enjoyment of his two visits in 1818 and 1844 – answered questions of mine about the troops at the Parade this morning and about Mrs. Pitt the wife of the Chaplain here of whom the dear Duchess and Baroness so often spoke – She was the great friend of the Empress Elizabeth and after the death of her husband the Empress gave her the rooms in the Winter Palace now occupied by Css. Bloudoff and where we go so often – The Emperor said that during Arthur's prayer, the thought had come across him that at the time of the events commemorated in the Hall where the Service took place – 1812, Russia had only one ally – England – and I told him how happy A. had been that that Hall had been the one chosen. I told him how much we had been interested in the Library, founded by Catherine and among other things, by a certain Volume in the library of Voltaire, bought entire by Her – written to prove that there was no Supreme Being or cause – and which Voltaire had carefully marked and noted with a view to refuting it, beginning his refutation on the first blank leaf with the words so often quoted 'Si Dieu n'existait pas il faudrait l'inventer.'

'Oh! yes' he said 'il n'etait pas Chrétien mais ce n'etait pas un athée.'

I said that A. was always so anxious that such people should be treated rather as mistaken friends than as enemies and he answered 'il a bien raison.' Apropos of the Nurse – he told of a Valet de Chambre Anglais who had been with the Emperor Alexander from his boyhood and who when too old for work, was treated quite like a friend and also lodged at Tsarkoe – he had a son who became an officer and was a passionate sportsman – even after leaving the Russian service and retiring to England, he used to come every winter to Russia to hunt bears and wolves and thinking it ungracious to take a dirty advantage of them by carrying a gun, he always went with a spear only and accompanied by one peasant! He has not been back for some years and the Emp: has heard nothing of him.

The Empress sent for Punch to shew us a picture of Punch giving his benediction to the pair and a cupid looking on in a bear's skin! –

January 27.

We went out at 9.30 with Major Cowell who had breakfasted with us and saw the curious little house of Peter the Great on the other side of the Neva, which is covered in and preserved like a relic. Peter built it and lived in it in order to watch from that vantage ground all work for the building of his new City and in it are preserved some specimens of his handicraft –

At 1 I again dressed for the reception. . . . Lady Emma and I found the dear young Grand Duchess in a most becoming toilette – All tulle and wreaths of little pink rose buds up the dress and the train – On the head the Gd. Duchess wore the Russian diadem, light pink, studded with diamonds – but not heavy and this with soft curly hair and the lovely rose bud complexion was exceedingly becoming – The Grand Duchess has a lovely neck and shoulders, and is altogether beautifully made – and tho' one can not (it is not fair to do so) call Her exactly pretty, the 'ensemble' is very charming.

She wore today the magnificent sapphires given by the

THE RUSSIAN MARRIAGE SERVICE OF THE DUKE AND DUCHESS OF
EDINBURGH IN ST. PETERSBURG

From a hitherto unpublished Drawing

Emperor yesterday, and which the Imperial family have been collecting ever since the birth of the Princess –

... 12 Peasants from the district of Smolensk were waiting to present a copy subscribed for in the District of which they were the elders, of a favorite and much esteemed Sacred picture, towards the purchase of this multitudes of the smallest coins were brought by even the very poor – Nothing could be nicer than the hearty, graceful, sensible, pleasant way in which the Grand Duchess spoke to all – we could not tell what she was saying – but the tone was enough to shew how excellent it was – The Peasants had tea in Countess Bloudoff's room afterwards – but first they carried the picture and put it themselves in H.I.H.'s rooms – and said how kind she was and how like the Emperor – and of the Duke, that he was 'quite like a Russian' which was of course, in their lips, a great compliment.

A few minutes before 8 Lord Sydney and I made our way to the Royal Box, or rather an ante room to it constructed over the Grand Staircase lined with Gobelins, and filled with Palms and trees of many kinds and with flowers – not only hyacinths – but roses, lilacs, lilies of the valley – it was like fairy land. The Great people began to arrive – then the Members of the Imperial Family and at last the Emperor with the Duke and Duchess – His Majesty passed thro' the room, greeting all most kindly and then leading the Gd. Duchess forward and making way for the Duke – H.M. drew back, while the whole house rose to receive them with the heartiest cheers. The Emperor's manner in putting forward the young couple and their own attitude were charming – The Streets on our way home were lighted up as if it had been day by the illuminations and were full of people standing to watch in the cold or driving in sledges – I hear that the Empress was in the Grand Duchess's room today before the reception and was feeling better and hoping to be able to be present at the Ball tomorrow – it must be a great trial to be unable to accompany the Emperor and Her Children and to be deprived by health of so much – I can not describe how kind the Emperor and Empress are and how beautifully everything is arranged and managed – how magnificent everything is, how every want is forestalled and how at home one feels –.

CHAPTER XII

Lady Augusta talks to the Empress. Moscow and festivities at the Kremlin. Moscow Society. St. Petersburg – farewell visits. The return to England, via Berlin.

CHAPTER XII

Lady Augusta to her sister.

Winter Palace, February 2, 1874.

On Saturday the 31st, I had for the first time a real talk
with the Empress. I was told to be there at 2. and came
back from luncheon at the Gd. Duchess Nicholas. . . .
She herself is an angel, so good and simple and devout and
so large hearted and liberal-minded. She is not very
happy, I should think, very homely looking and married
to the handsomest of the late Emperor's sons – She
speaks rather sadly of life – but she said that to have lived
to see the liberating of the Serfs, was to have experienced
a joy which outweighed much sorrow –

The Empress spoke of everything – we were alone – said
how warmly the Pss. of Wales spoke of the Queen's kindness and of Her as a model mother-in-law. – then of the
relations between Mother and children. I took it for
granted that there had been many mistakes but insisted
much on the good intentions and spoke a good deal of the
circumstances altogether. She did not press me, nor give
a sign of blame or doubt, only I thought it would give her
confidence if I took for granted that I knew she *must* have
heard and then appuyé much on the good. – I said how
nice, how simple, how completely unspoiled [the Queen]

was in the way of being puffed up by position, du reste I added. 'Y.M. knows by the Emperor how certain natures can go thro' such ordeals without losing anything of their simplicity – the only thing is that a person brought up in such exceptional position, and alone, can not know the world as others do and can not buy their experience or acquire it from seeing others, and may be doubly liable to make mistakes –'

She said that all she begged was that the Queen should say directly to her, herself, with perfect frankness and sincerity, anything She wishes altered. Her daughter had been accustomed to have everything said thus to her and knew quite how to take all such observations, if only the Q. would treat her with that perfect frankness and directness – and then She said, when that is so, as it ought to be between parents and children, all is easy and there is no interference 'elle se conforme et je n'admets pas que l'on ait le droit de critiquer les Parents.'

It was so good and kind and true and wise and oh! if only H.M. would learn that now, and for others! –

The Empress said of course between Husband and Wife, à Dieu ne plaise, that anyone should ever interfere. 'Avant le mariage tant que l'on veut on peut tout leur faire – mais après cela est fini j'ai dit a ma fille et à A Maintenant si vous vous trouvex des défauts il faut tâcher de les corriger ou de suppléer à ce qui manque, mais gardez cela pour vous et supportez-le et ne le dites jamais' –

It was very very charming – She coughed a good deal and looked very weak, but so calm and self controlled –

He came in, his big black dog bounding at his side, in

joy at the prospect of a walk – he had made a rush for the Grand Duchess's door, so confident was he that she must be one of the party!

When he told this, I could hardly keep from crying.

Today (Feb: 3) I saw her again and she coughed less – they say she is calmer and better since Her sacrifice est fait – She seems very much touched by the Queen's love and tenderness and has no fear, neither has the Grand Duchess, of getting on. The Empress was most kind – wishes to see us on our way from Moscow home and much invites us to come back another time to St. P. She gave me a lovely bracelet and was very sweet.

The dear Duke of Oldenberg is delicious. 'Thank God I have a body of highly respectable females, 1500 teachers, thank God, highly respectable.'

Talking of his son's marriage, 'He was in a garrison town and married without telling me – very wrong, highly wrong – he was taken in, poor devil, but thank God it has turned out better than one could have hoped – a highly respectable female.'

His other dear little daughter in law described a part of his care, was to form what you call wet nurses, but his own account of it was that in London *'not for love nor money'* could he or his poor Wife find a midwife.

The Grand Duchess Marie is quite exquisite – so amusing . . . I roared yesterday at the Loftus ball. She was talking to Mr. Colville [1] and Emma – suddenly I saw the latter colour, and approached. She had been recounting to Mr. Colville that she had asked the Bride 'à quand le premier enfant?' and that She had answered ' "Je ne suis

[1] *Master of the Household to the Duke of Edinburgh and brother-in-law of Lady Frances Baillie.*

227

pas pressée mais A est très impatient," et elle a dit cela gentiment.'

I believe W.C. hardly followed at first, 'quoi, quoi?' he said, in a surprised tone. But he had I think, recovered when I saw him.

'Moi, voyez vous j'ai eu mon premier enfant 15 jours avant les neuf mois je n'étais pas honteuse, j'étais ravie, ravie. J'en ai eu huite et le dernier quand j'avais 42 ans et j'en étais plus folle que du premier' –

I believe W.C. had put in a few searching questions between. All at once she turned to Emma and said 'Ah! mon Dieu je ne devrais pas parler de ces choses devant une demoiselle, pardon, pardon' –

'Oh Mm. je n'ai rien compris, cela ne fait rien!!!'

It might have been less folichon not to have done it to an officer of the Guards!!!

Arthur went to luncheon there today – I was sent for by the Empress and could not go – She was most serious and charming. . . .

I think my evening dresses needlessly heavy and elaborate – very handsome but I should have been happier with two whites, much less elaborate – These endless passages and floors trodden by thousands of servants and soldiers blacken these long heavy gowns in *one wearing*. [Mr. Colville] has a growing opinion of the Bride, and her mother also, but all will depend on how [the Duke] uses his influence. Mary [her maid] says he is so nice, stands watching her train being done etc., 'reminds her of Master James, how he would watch his Mama!!!'[1]

[1] *Mary had been Lady Frances Baillie's maid and James was Lady Frances' son.*

MOSCOW

Train to Moscow. Feb. 4.

... I feel I have done quite well, and my diamonds
have struck terror into all beholders, though really here,
one almost gets tired of them – The Grand Duchesses are
literally covered with them – belts, trimmings, skirts,
bodies, heads – gigantic stones – and emeralds, and other
stones besides. My rings appear on every occasion, the big
one caught the lynx eye of the ladies and produced the
greatest impression. The Gros. Crescent stars and ear
rings are disposed ornamentally on my person each time I
dress – and the Greek Cross is never absent. . . . There is
never a Ball without a sitting down supper, which is a
terrible tax and bother and the supper is like a dinner –
only imagine what a supper of 2000, as at the Palace,
must have been?

I should think that no one could go into Society
at all without carriages and immense appliances of
every sort – even young girls wear such expensive
clothes. . . .

We slept sound in this comfortable cabin [on the train]
till 11.30 when we were called to breakfast with the suite.
What was my horror on entering the salle to find an
immense table – the Emperor, Grand Dukes, the couple
and all the party – I was all fuzzy and half asleep and
quite confounded! – Breakfast did us good however, and
on the strength of it I am making this attempt to write.
The train runs smoothly.

The snow is falling heavily and one sees fir trees and
occasional wooden houses of peasants. They cheer the
Emperor at the stations.

The young couple look bright and nice and happy and
they all talked merrily at breakfast at their end – She is

not pretty exactly, but very pleasant looking and has a very frank, pleasing manner. . . .

Sclavonik Bazar, Moscow, Feb. 5.

A dreadful rumour, apparently well authenticated, reached the Princess of Wales' ladies, that we must all appear this morning at the Kremlin at 10.30 in trains and feathers! – At 2 a.m. we held a consultation and I wrote Cts. Tolstoy a note, to be dispatched the first thing this morning. Owing to the confusion of tongues, altho' the name of 'Lord Stanley' is written up over our door – I never received the answer and at 10.15 was still sitting unclothed, when a peremptory summons came from the gentlemen that we were to appear, dead or alive. – It was morning dress and bonnet after all, so we had only the fright. –

On reaching the Salle d'attente, I was introduced to 12 more 'demoiselles a cheffre' whose names remain a perfect blank till this hour to me. –

It usually happens that when I next meet one of these new acquaintances they say 'Veuillez me nommez à Lady Osborne,' the one thing it is quite out of my power to do. –

The Grand Duchess looked very charming, though a little pale from all this fatigue, and again spoke with the greatest pleasantness and naturel apropos to those who brought offerings. – Whether they were humble donors of bread and salt and dishes of 'sterlits,' a favourite fish caught in the Volga and a national dish (two of which were brought alive in a sort of bath) or to Nobles of Moscow who presented the most gorgeous casket weighing forty pounds, of pure gold and worked in the admirable

style for which the workmen of Moscow are famed. . . .
When the Grand Duchess came out of her apartments
today for the 'Baise Mains,' we went up one staircase, and
the Royal couple took another. At the top there was the
Duke, sad and disconsolate, what had happened or would
happen?

In a few seconds the flooring, a large square of it, slowly
rose and slowly and noiselessly, a glass case emerged, in
the centre of which, standing erect, resplendent with gold
and precious stones, in the beautiful white and dark blue
Russian Court dress, appeared the smiling face and the
pretty figure of the dear Grand Duchess.

It was quite like a fairy tale. –

. . . In the Museum, among crowds of most curious
and interesting relics, we came once more on Queen
Elizabeth, in the shape of a carriage sent by Her to John
the Terrible, and later of a letter of congratulation
written to the same on his accession and begging that an
unfortunate English doctor might be allowed to return
to his Country.

On February 6th, was the State dinner in the Vladimir
Hall of the Kremlin. Dean Stanley described the scene,
'magnificently lighted, and at the chief table, where the
Emperor sat, the plate consisted of ancient flagons and
plates and ornaments, all English (with the exception of
two or three Danish, out of compliment to the Prince of
Denmark and the Cesarevna), presents to the former
Czars from Elizabeth, James I., and Charles I., – the
Danish ones from Christian IV. Augusta sat between the
Prince of Wales and the Duke of Coburg, I between the
Greek Minister and Countess Tolstoy.'

Lady Augusta to her sister.

Kremlin, Feb. 10.

The snow was driving sharply as we went and returned in our sledge – all the ladies wear Russian Shetland Shawls tied over their hats and round their necks – Once or twice I have felt here a sharp pain in my forehead from the cold, I could hardly have believed how sharp it could be –

. . . On Saturday morning we went to the Kremlin and under their guidance, visited what remained to be seen – The Chief Halls and apartments are what we should call on the second floor and as we walked thro' them, they were flooded with the bright beautiful sunlight. . . . Issuing from one of the beautiful Halls . . . was the entrance to that portion of the old palace . . . now restored, according to descriptions and drawings, to as nearly as possible its ancient condition. The low small rooms leaving one to wonder how a family could have lived in them. . . . In these apartments, if one may dignify them with such a name, were some very interesting antiquities, autographs and manuscripts etc. Among the latter, an illustrated account of the election and coronation of the first Romanoff . . . an invaluable historical document – We saw the 'trésor' of the Cathedral with very interesting historical relics and ecclesiastical treasures of countless price 'gold and silver, and precious stones.' – One of the curious things is the apartment containing the gigantic cauldron in which the holy oil, to serve for the whole Russian Church, is prepared at Easter time, once in two years, and the array of silver jars of large size in which it is kept till required. It is fragrant till you smell too closely, when the original odour of lamp oil becomes apparent. . . .

We visited the three Cathedrals – the Coronation, the Marriage – the Sepulchral Cathedral – always in company with the Priests – the one who watches over the resting place of the terrible Ivan, on whose tomb even, one looks with considerable shrinking and awe – is a very able and pleasant man – he had been in the navy I think, and is outspoken and frank; they are very picturesque with their long hair and beards.

We found a crowd waiting patiently outside the little house where we took tea – one friend asked what they were waiting for, and they replied, 'The Emperor' –! At every available spot in and about Moscow they were on the look out for H.M., who, when we told Him, seemed only to regret that he could not be ubiquitous –

February 12th.

One of the Slavs is Pr. Tcherkassky, an excellent and clever man with a very charming wife, delicate, modest, 'faisant valoir les autres' – He holds a high office in Poland and was much liked. She lent me some articles on the Polish question – the idea is that 'Poland and Russia cannot exist as equals. One must rule the other, history, experience, geography, prove it.'

. . . Of course we reason on the improbability of separating from Ireland in something of the same absolute way, but there is no such hatred on the part of the conquerors. Still, Tcherkassky was much liked and thought very fair and just. He was recalled on some Russian complaint – Government servants in Russia are very liable to being recalled without knowing the reason why –

Ld. A. Loftus speaks of great corruption still, up to the very steps of the throne, and is very pompous and mysterious [1] –

Another guest was Soloviøff. All these are remnants of the old Slav Society which was so distinguished – they have a little out lived their grievances and their 'raison d'être' – Soloviøff is the Historian of Russia – his extremely voluminous work is still in progress – Karamsine was his predecessor – his work is still much read – this is more documentary and rather tedious for the general reader – I met at M. Ozeroff's, the daughter of Karamsine. She is a thorough going Russ. – no longer young – would have been or would be a Jeanne d'Arc, only I see no probability of the independence of Russia being menaced!!!

. . . Mme. Aksakoff [who had been governess to the Grand Duchess] is a more cultivated person and a person of more depth of mind than Css. Tolstoy, clever tho' the latter is, but she was less a woman of the world and the one, from want of knowledge and the other, from want of grace and refinement of manner, have allowed their pupil to grow up walking badly and the like – Mme. Aksakoff was much pleased with the Duke of E. and his manner to his Wife – She is, I am sure, an excellent friend to her and has remained on intimate terms, corresponding frequently – She is very anxious for her good and that she may be guided and developed and learn to know and value England and be known and valued there.

. . . Another sister is Maid of Honour. She has, up a

[1] '*This judgment of Lord A. Loftus was shared by Lord Granville who found him "terribly pompous and tiresome."*' *He wrote to the Queen when Lord A. Loftus was Ambassador in Berlin, that Lord A. Loftus had been to see him at the F.O., 'and harangued Lord Granville for an hour without the latter being able to get in a word.' – The Queen's Letters.*

THE KREMLIN

very high stair, a lovely room looking out on the Place
Alexandre, to which access is gained thro' galleries and
passages still a labyrinth to me, but not so awfully smelly
and dirty as the downstairs passages and little staircase of
which access is gained to the rooms of my 'Nadine.'
Some of the gentlemen maintain that they got to know
where they were by the smell – I quite believe it and I
again say how the ladies can look as they do coming thro'
such dirty passages, I cannot understand – 'Essence of
Cossack' – 'Bouquet of Priobi-jensky,' 'Les Chevaliers
Gardes' etc., etc., and thro' and beyond and between
them all, the ever present flavour of the unadulterated
Mujik. – The third sister, Kitty Tutcheff, is not very
handsome but she is charming – She was a great friend of
the Metropolitan Philarete. In her anxiety to make him
known and to spread the good of his Sermons, she undertook to translate them into English, with the help of the
only teacher she could procure at the time – a 'ci devant
Zouave'! not a very literary, still less a very theological
character – her Sister's description of the struggle over
this labour of love and the iron will that conquered the
difficulties and resolutely kept the Zouave within bounds,
which she did all but one, when, after long efforts, a fit
of 'fou rire' overcame him at the extraordinary folly, as
it seemed to him, of the subject and the language – it was
some Schoolman's disquisition on a most intricate question, relating to the Blessed Virgin! He could not recover
his gravity and the 'séance' had to be 'suspendue' –

. . . Another old lady who at nearly 90 does not miss a
Ball, is the Mother of a Princess Troubetzkoy who took
me to see the cheaper lodging houses which she and others
have built – They are excellent people and I enjoyed

myself much in talking to her, at the Balls – they had all ardently desired the abolition of Serfage – she described that the effect among others had been to compel landlords to live more on their estates as they have to 'faire valoir.' . . . Pss. T. says she would gladly go abroad in winter, but she could not bear to lose her summer in the Country.

The relations between them and their former serfs are very pleasant. – there is much more affection and respect. . . . The men of the Imperial Family seem to shew very great respect in all they are called on to do – and yet one knows that some of them are not what we should call God fearing. . . .

Later.

. . . Today we have seen the Grand Duchess Iblene's Institution of Sisters of Charity, which delighted me. . . . One of the doctors invited me to see a sister extract teeth, which she does admirably. Then we went to see the cheap dinners for the poor, something like those at Glasgow. . . . All was excellent till we came to the Russian porridge. In an unwary moment I tasted it, and I think I shall taste it to my dying day. I can only suppose that lamp oil was the ingredient used to give it the desired flavour and succulence.

St. Petersburgh. Feb. 13.

We dined at the Station with the Imperial party and saw them off and then returned to the Hotel where 3 or 4 of the old friends came to talk till bed time – We had in the train some charming conversation with the Prince of Denmark – he is very superior – so modest – so thoughtful, so serious and so amiable.

The Crown Princess was much pleased with Moscow,

and left a delightful impression there, from the interest
H.R.H. took in all things and Her activity and zeal –

They drove to the Monastery of Semenoff where
they showed us into the Refectoire and some soup was
brought, but when I looked at the bearer, and the thought
flashed across me of what the ideas of cleanliness could
be in a kitchen presided over by such a being, and from
whence proceeded such odours, I could not have tasted
it to save my life, I think. – The filth of these hereditary
sheepskin coats is something 'phenomenal' – we dined
with Cts. Dobrinsky, a pleasant family dinner, and then
made most ridiculous attempts to call on friends. No one
knows any address in Russia, and in Moscow no one
seemed to know any road or street. When, after being
repulsed at many wrong doors, we at length reached our
destination and were ushered upstairs, and had divested
ourselves of the clothing that was to keep out 20 degrees
of cold, – we found the Lady we came to visit, *out*!!

Off we started again, up hill, and down dale, – we told
them where to go for the next address, the carriage
stopped, much conversation ensued and off we went, as
we fondly believed, to our longed for goal. Again the
whole process was gone through! and this time we found
ourselves 'face to face' with a lady on whom we had *no*
intention of calling!

We took a sorrowful farewell of our rooms in the Kremlin and the exquisite view, and went once more on one of
those astonishing voyages of discovery, up and down the
streets – to dinner at our friend's house and then to the
train. – We had a comfortable compartment to ourselves
with a ventilator, but this the Guard, by coughing
violently and going through many pantomimic scenes, at

length persuaded me to close (at least for a time). At intervals in the night, he came to impress upon me sundry most important facts and opinions. The Dean he thought hopeless, but he never gave me up – and evidently thought that by talking long enough and at last, almost *into* my ear – a ray of intelligence might be kindled in me – the only word that produced this magic effect on me was 'tea.' To that, I ever responded and the more gladly as it delivered me from my devoted, but rather oppressive friend –

When they left Russia, the Dean wrote:

'The glorious dream is over. The most splendid certainly, and one of the most interesting passages of my life. . . . Sunday preached in the mg. in Pr. Oldenburg's Lutheran Chapel and in the afternoon, a farewell sermon to many English and Russians in the English Church. – In the evg. an immense state dinner in the Palace for the Emperor of Austria – We spoke for the last time to the Emperor and Empress and I saw quite close, but was not introduced to the Emperor of Austria – older and plainer than I expected. A far more interesting person in appearance was Ct. Andrassy, his Prime Minister, in Hungarian dress, with the black locks and handsome face of a romantic bandit.

'Monday I went to the Alexander Nevsky Convent once more – first to address a few words in French to the students, to which one replied. It was very deeply affecting to me – the thought that these were the only words that they had ever heard or were likely to hear from a stranger. . . . Then, by invitation of the Metropolitan of St. P. whose fête day it was, I breakfasted or dined at a

State banquet where were all the chief lay and ecclesiastical dignitaries connected with the Church. The 3 Metropolitans were opposite me. When the banquet was over,
after the usual toasts of the Emperor, the Holy Synod,
and the Metropolitan, the Metropolitan rose (and quite
without precedent, they said) proposed the "D. of West.
and the Church of England, as represented in him" and
begged me to convey his salutations to the Archp. of
Canterbury – He also gave me a Russian Prayerbook in
commemoration of the day.

'. . . On the morning of Tuesday we took a last drive
in bright sunshine in the sledge down to the Neva – and
then took a drive in a sledge, with the Laplanders and the
Reindeer. It was deeply affecting to take the last farewell
– some of them came to the station – one as far as the first
station on the way. We watched all the signs of Russia –
as long as we could. Peasants, wooden houses – gilded
cupolas, fields of snow. At last all melted away and we
are here again, in the common life of Europe.'

CHAPTER XIII

In Berlin, with the Crown Prince and Princess. The Duke of Edinburgh and his bride arrive in England. Lady Augusta's illness. Life resumed at the Deanery. The Czar in England. The Dean on Church affairs in a letter to the Queen. Letters from Madame Mohl. Annie Besant and Dean Stanley. Lady Augusta and the Duchess of Kent's Journal. The Duchess of Kent's relations with the Queen. Lady Augusta's continued illness and her search for a cure in France.

Q

CHAPTER XIII

1874.

Lady Augusta and the Dean stayed in Berlin, on the way back to England. At Berlin, they dined one day

'with the Crown Prince and Princess – the next with them only and Pss. Hermann Hohenlohe at the Emperor and Empress's – She quite well again – the day after with Odo Russells – and last day with the Bancrofts [the American Minister] – one evening we spent at Bismarck's very interesting – he talked to me a great deal at Supper about his own life and work – as relating to his health he was very cheery.'

Back in England, Lady Augusta found an accumulation of work and worry at Westminster and, from the rich and exciting experiences of Russia, she was thrown into a succession of duties too much for her strength, for she was ill and tired. When they arrived in England the Queen was in London, and on the first night they were summoned to Her, finding her impatient for every detail of the adventure and ceremony in Russia.

Lady Augusta was ill for a week, and from then her story becomes that of a fight against weakness and approaching death. People who remember her say that she worked twice as hard as anybody about her, that her life was such a splendid and unselfish service for her Queen

243

and everybody about her, that her body simply failed to serve the astonishing energy of her mind and heart.

Her voluminous letters are proof of this energy, for she wrote to everybody, it seems. She was adviser and friend to her Queen, ministering angel to the poor of Westminster, and, between these calls on her time, writer of countless letters to her family and to every unhappy and tormented soul whose friend and guardian she became.

The Duke of Edinburgh and his Russian Princess arrived in England in March, and the Dean and Lady Augusta, the latter coming from her sick-bed, went down to Windsor.

'We saw the Queen and all the family (except Pr. Arthur, who had gone to meet the comers at Gravesend), drive out through the Park, down a long Avenue of Guards.'

Windsor was beautiful on that March day, with the Long Walk, leading to the Castle, alive with the first green of spring. There was 'a crowd of boys from the great School of Eton.'

'The Queen and her daughter-in-law stepped out first, and as soon as they passed inside the doors, she kissed her most warmly . . . the Grand Duchess looked full of radiance in her new home. . . . The Queen was delighted.'

Lady Augusta dined at Windsor that night. She wrote to her sister:

'The Russian friends were delighted to see us – delighted with the reception, delighted with Windsor. We dined that evening, no one but the Pair, Princes Arthur and Leopold and Princess Beatrice. . . . Two of the Russians. . . . The Duchess quite at ease. We were all presented to the Duchess in the corridor by the Queen, as soon as we got up the staircase.'

The Queen was 'quite nervous and trembling,' as She herself wrote in her Journal. 'Marie, who is very like her photographs, wore a light blue dress with a long train and a white tulle bonnet with white roses and white heather, which I had purposely sent to Antwerp in the yacht. . . . Dear Marie has a very friendly manner, a pleasant face, beautiful skin and fine bright eyes, and there is something very fresh and attractive about her. She speaks English wonderfully well.'

Lady Augusta forced herself into a full life, in spite of her weakness, and she received the Ladies of the Russian Court at Westminster. On one such day, she wrote to the Queen:

'Princess Wiosenesky and Prince Baryatinsky came to Luncheon and to go over the Abbey yesterday – it was a great pleasure to hear them express the thankfulness they felt for the reception their darling Princess had met with – and the joy with which they look forward to telling the Empress all that will comfort and lighten Her want. – The Princess and Mme. Ozeroff dine with us on Tuesday.'

Her sister, Lady Frances Baillie, was appointed Lady-in-Waiting to the Duchess of Edinburgh, and Lady Augusta wrote to the Queen:

'This evening, Fanny goes to her waiting with great interest and pleasure.'

Continuing her letter to the Queen, she wrote:

'We have been greatly troubled by a sad accident to a dear old woman of 85 whom we met and were much struck with two or three years ago in the Abbey. – She fell and broke *both her arms* on Saturday – Her patience and submission are quite wonderful and to see the active, lively spirit thus imprisoned, and the poor suffering body lying so *perfectly* helpless, and to hear her yet praising and thanking God and seeing Love and Mercy in all His dealings, is a great lesson – She described to us, with much fire and poetry, a sort of dream or vision she had had many months ago – and spoke of a light which was not like the light of stars, but more the white light which *she had been told* that diamonds gave out!! –

'She had never seen a diamond!

'I thought it would have interested Your Majesty very much to have seen and heard one in whom the spirit so triumphed over the flesh!'

To the Queen.

April 20.

. . . I am so delighted to hear how much the Duchess of Edinburgh has admired and enjoyed Osborne and to think of the fine days there. . . .

The Abbey yesterday was again crowded from end to end, by people of all classes and all denominations. – I hope to enclose the printed paper of the Service. There was a dear old Sister of Dr. Livingstone's who thanked the Dean in very broad Scotch and a very choking voice! – . . .

I can not resist sending Your Majesty a note, to be burnt, containing the apology, or rather, the cry of

anguish of the Reporters of the 'Standard' who in a weak
moment asked the Dean for the MS. of his Sermon and
promised to lend it to the other Reporters, little knowing
what they asked for!!!!!

The Czar himself came to England in May, 'terribly
altered, so thin, and his face looks so old, sad and care-
worn,' wrote the Queen in her Journal.

And then, Windsor settled down to the old routine,
with Disraeli making frequent visits to the Castle, and
the Dean at Westminster answering the unending questions of the Queen. On June the 14th, he wrote to
Her:

'The Dean of Westminster presents his humble duty to
Your Majesty. He obeys the Queen's command by writing a few words on the position of Church affairs.

'Perhaps the Queen would like to hear his opinion on
the Scottish Patronage Bill. – He certainly agrees with
Lord Grey and Lord Camperdown that it would have
been much better to have allowed the whole parish,
certainly the heritors to have a voice in nominating the
ministers. – The Duke of Argyll made a very able and
dogmatic speech for the other side – but the Dean cannot
agree with him, as the Duke knows, and therefore, he
hopes, will not be offended if the Dean tells Your Majesty
of a dream which the Duke assures the Dean that he really
dreamed at Inverness; where his thoughts, as the Queen
will understand, were divided between his study of
natural history, and his anxiety about patronage. – He
dreamed one night that he had hit on the best mode
of electing the Ministers. It was that they should be

appointed by the *singing birds, throstles, blackbirds, linnets, larks, etc.*, and he said to himself "This will do very well – and I think also that it will satisfy the Dean of Westminster." – But then, just as he was waking – a voice seemed to say to him – "No – it will not satisfy the Dean at all; for he will insist on adding the eagles, vultures, crows, hawks, owls and ravens. –" and so he woke – . The Dean thinks that the voice was quite right. For the Minister of a parish has to look after all the people in the place, and not only those who are of his own ways of thinking and those who are communicants. And there the crows and hawks have as much a right and have as great an interest in having a good Minister as the throstles and linnets.

'The Queen will not (the Dean hopes) disapprove of the part which he took in the unveiling of the statue of Bunyan which was given to the town of Bedford by the Duke of Bedford. It was a very interesting occasion – and it was delightful to see the pleasure which was given to quite the humblest classes by seeing this honor paid to one whose writings were so familiar to themselves. The Dissenters are at this time very unreasonable and uncharitable – But the Dean thinks that this is an additional reason for trying to soften their prejudices by taking part in anything where he can express sympathy with them, whilst at the same time it gives him the opportunity of saying to them a few words of wholesome truth.

'He then went to Leicester to preach for the youngest brother of Dr. Vaughan – and visited with much interest the beautiful park of Bradgate, where took place the well known scene of Lady Jane Grey reading Plato, whilst the others were hunting.'

LETTER FROM MADAME MOHL

Madame Mohl to Lady Augusta.

Paris, March, *1874.*

Dearest,

I have just finished reading, or rather boggling, over your letter, and so rejoiced was I that I wrote yesterday such a candid and beautiful picture of my own virtues and merits that there is nothing more to be said, except that as I should have had much delight in your descriptions, hot and hot like a beef-steak at *Dolly's* (ancient days), so I promised myself never more to be good, virtuous, or self-denying – c'est un métier de dupe. We have been worse than dull this last month, instead of these assumptions of yours. These deaths cast such a gloom over me that I never invited a soul all March, and scarcely went out. The poor Lyttons, whom I saw often and intimately, lost their only boy, two years old – one or two days' illness. They were so cut up they ran away to England, to hide themselves like wounded hares. I did so pity them. Then M. Guizot lost his daughter. I saw him six days after that event. He was calm and collected. Alluding to his age, he said a death was but a short separation; that he felt more for the husband than he could express; that their union had been a happiness for twenty-two years, and that few who died could have had such a destiny. His power of work goes on, and that is his salut He wishes ardently to finish his 'History of France.' It is very touching to see the old man of eighty-six or eighty-seven working hard. When I saw him he was at his desk as busy as possible.

Forgive this horrid scribble; I have not time to copy it.

Yours ever,

MARY MOHL

Later when Madame Mohl was in England, staying at Cold Overton:

Dearest Friend,

I regret missing Dr. Temple very much – his conversation would never grow cold, because it leaves a movement in one's head. One of my nieces tells me he is Bishop of Exeter, for I had forgotten it, and, as he wrote in 'Essays and Reviews,' I am astonished that he is. I did not think there was so much sense in the appointments to bishoprics.

Our wedding went off yesterday very well, but I am shocked to see the absurd luxury of such useful and, in fact, indispensable operations as weddings. The breakfast sent from Leicester, with waiters, etca, would have nourished a whole parish for a week with good wholesome food, instead of kickshaws (taken from the French quelquechose); and in the primitive old-fashioned house it looked to me like a respectable lady dressed out en Venus with cupids and doves. I was exceedingly glad when it was all over, and the gathering dispersed this morning.

Tell Arthur I have finished 'Lord Minto,' and shall write my satisfaction to the writer, who is wonderfully pretty to write such a clever book, too. I was not ennuyed on my journey, for Lady Galway was on the platform, and came into my carriage, leaving her spouse alone, and we talked all the way. She was very entertaining.

When you have settled where you go and when, pray let me know, and the probabilities of your continental flights and studies of old France. Love to Arthur, and many thanks for the loan of the book.

Yours ever, dear kind friend,

MARY MOHL.

The shadow of Lady Augusta's illness lengthened and depressed the life and energies of the Deanery. The Dean was at 'the culminating point' in his career. Archbishop Tait said of him, that he was a 'power, not only in the Church, but in the world.' He had made the Abbey a 'centre of religious and national life.' But the companion of that fame, the graceful, human, yet saintly wife, was slowly dying. Lady Welby wrote of 'the sunshine of her smile and the keen sense of joy and the power of enjoyment,' but most of all, of the 'faultlessness of her impulses. Quicker than thought, she would choose the right – it was like the needle to the pole. Thus she required no rules to live by, but followed unerringly the voice of the Lord within her . . . her marvellous power of entering into the sufferings of those who, without any dangerous illness, were continually tormented by a morbid sensitiveness which made even trifles well-nigh insupportable.'

About this time, an extraordinary service was asked of the Dean by Mrs. Annie Besant, and the record of it gives an interesting sidelight on the character of the life at Westminster, which was shared by both husband and wife. Mrs. Annie Besant tells the story. She writes:

'My dear mother had an intense longing to take the Sacrament, but absolutely refused to do so unless I partook of it with her.

' "If it is necessary to Salvation," she persisted doggedly, "I will not take it if darling Annie is to be shut out. I would rather be lost with her than saved without her."

'In vain I urged that I could not take it, without telling the officiating clergyman of my heresy, and that under such circumstances, the clergyman would be sure to refuse to administer it to me. She insisted that she could not die happy if she did not take it with me. I went to a clergyman I knew well, and laid the case before him; as I expected, he refused to allow me to communicate. I tried a second, the result was the same. I was in despair.

'At last a thought struck me; there was Dean Stanley, my mother's favourite, a man known to be of the broadest school within the Church of England; suppose I asked him? I did not know him, though as a young child, I had known his sister as my mother's friend, and I felt the request would be something of an impertinence. Yet there was just the chance that he might consent, and then my darling's death-bed would be the easier. I told no one, but set out resolutely for the Deanery, Westminster, timidly asked for the Dean, and followed the servant upstairs with a very sinking heart. I was left for a moment alone in the library, and then the Dean came in.

'Very falteringly I preferred my request, stating baldly that I was not a believer in Christ, that my mother was dying, that she was fretting to take the Sacrament, that she would not take it unless I took it with her, that two clergymen had refused to allow me to take part in the service, that I had come to him in despair, feeling how great was the intrusion – but she was dying.

' "You were quite right to come to me," he said, as I concluded; "of course I will go and see your mother, and I have little doubt that if you will not mind talking over your position with me we may see our way clear to doing as your mother wishes."

'I could hardly speak my thanks, so much did the kindly sympathy move me, the revulsion from the anxiety and

fear of rebuff was strong enough to be almost pain. But
Dean Stanley did more than I asked. He suggested that
he should call that afternoon, and have a quiet chat with
my mother and then come on the following day to administer the Sacrament.

'"A stranger's presence is always trying to a sick
person," he said, with rare delicacy of thought, "and,
joined to the excitement of the service, it might be too
much for your dear mother. If I spend half an hour with
her today, and administer the Sacrament tomorrow, it
will, I think, be better for her."

'So Dean Stanley came that afternoon, and remained
talking with my mother for about half an hour, and then
set himself to understand my own position.

'On the following day he came again, and celebrated
the "Holy Communion" by the bedside of my dear
mother. Well was I repaid for the struggle it had cost me
to ask so great a kindness from a stranger, when I saw the
comfort that gentle, noble heart had given to my mother.'

Lady Augusta's last grand service for the Queen had a
curious and lovely link with her first association with the
Court and, towards the end of 1874, when she rested as
much as possible at Westminster, she edited and arranged
the Journals of the Duchess of Kent, to whom she had gone
as a young girl, from Paris. The story of the Bruces'
service to the Court opened, no doubt, when the Dowager
Lady Elgin, mother of Thomas Lord Elgin, famous for his
association with the marbles of the Parthenon, became
Governess to Princess Charlotte. Her son was brought to
the King as a little boy. When he gave up, his own children by his second marriage all came to form some

service of friendship with the Victorian Court. Lady Augusta had made Frogmore her home and the Duchess of Kent, sad and old and destined to be misunderstood by so many historians, was a second mother to her. So this last work of editing 'the sacred journals' was as great a pleasure to her as it was an honour on the part of the Queen, for the journals were to be destroyed and only extracts retained. They refute the tradition (still fostered by those who like their history to be melodramatic rather than true) that the Duchess and the Queen maintained a strained and suspicious relationship, when the Princess left Kensington Palace to become Queen at Windsor. That the Duchess of Kent was misled in choosing her advisers may be true. The Queen, whose instinct for good people and honest people was unerring, dismissed the Irishman Conroy from Her mother's service. He had never been more or less than an intimate adviser, and those perverted historians who suggest the contrary cannot produce one document to prove their vulgar suggestion.

But the Duchess accepted the position, acknowledged her daughter's judgment and never, as Lady Augusta's earlier letters show, allowed a prejudice or a bitterness to remain. If she had an outlet for otherwise hidden resentments, she would have chosen her private Journals, in which she wrote, even in the last days when her arms were stiff and in agony. She wished those Journals destroyed, but the Queen read them and entrusted them to Lady Augusta, who made extracts from them. The letters she wrote to the Queen about this time, show how the Duchess recovered from the first effects of the ill-chosen advisers, and one letter proves that both mother and daughter allowed love to conquer a small difference and enrich the relationship during the long years when the Duchess lived at Frogmore, with Lady Augusta as her Lady-in-Waiting. Lady Augusta wrote to the Queen on August the 19th, referring first to her niece's toothache. But she

'would not leave the dear journals. Uncle Arthur undertook to take her to have the tooth extracted, under laughing gas! He acquitted himself of his duty beautifully and managed to read great part of a novel of the Prime Minister's, while waiting for the completion of the preparations!!

'The marriage of Lord Pembroke took place in the Abbey today – in Henry VII's Chapel – it was very quiet, very solemn, and very impressive and I trust, will be happy. It seems fitting that two such historical names should be united within those venerable, historical walls. It would be difficult to see anything more "goodly to look upon" than those two couples, the Brownlows and the Pembrokes.'·

Talking of the Duchess of Kent's journals, towards the close of the letter, she wrote:

'It has been so great an interest and so affecting a pleasure to trace the outline of that dear life, able as I am, to fill in so much of the detail and to live over again so many happy years, that I shall quite miss the quiet hours that I have spent with them.

'. . . These contain, as Your Majesty knows, dry daily facts, and the few purely personal remarks which enable one to trace, by inference, the touching inward and outward struggle, thro' which that devoted sensitive, maternal heart regained the peace and joy and confidence that had been destroyed by the timidity which allowed third persons to come between mother and child. . . . The struggle also against the irritation and despondency produced by physical suffering, a struggle unflinchingly maintained, and victoriously.

'The only sorrow the beloved Duchess's heart could not have struggled against; that Spirit, living only in love and in the welfare of others, could not have outlived the loss of Your Majesty's happiness. It must comfort and soothe Your Majesty to feel how entirely the tenderness of Your Majesty and the Prince brightened the declining years of that loving Mother. In the agony connected with the death of Prince Leiningen, this comfort appears in every word and these manifestations are dealt upon, even when the records are the briefest.

'. . . How childlike and beautiful and simple and transparent a Soul – The Dear Baroness used always to say that the Duchess had preserved the *religion* and delicacy of conscience and *simplicity* of a child. – . . . I think that the beloved Duchess was never quite at home with English sermons and services. . . . It will be a terrible wrench to destroy the Volumes, but Your Majesty will be strengthened if it is carrying out a wish.

'. . . We had another interesting visitor on Thursday, "Alfonso de Borbon," as he wrote his name. – He is an intelligent looking youth, well taught, knowing history, but not perhaps looking as if there was much originality or individuality to come. But he is very young and excellent manners and sufficient instruction at his age is a great deal. We gave him coffee in the Jerusalem Chamber and I did my best to warn him against the vacillation and want of straightforwardness and courage of poor Charles I.

'I thought I must for once sacrifice my dear Stuarts in the interests of Spain and of Europe, in case this Bourbon ever comes to the throne!! He spoke in a most Constitutional and chivalrous tone! Two nights ago, we took Constance Hamilton . . . and invaded dear old Carlyle at 11 p.m.

'We found him alone. A fire! The window open – the coffee pot by the fire and plenty of light, and he at once entered upon subject after subject, with his usual interest and strength. Presently the door opened and in came his niece, a slight, pretty, fairy looking little maiden of about 17 or 18, apparently. Quite at home with him, enjoying his talk and evidently having a good deal of weight in the family councils! The whole scene was most picturesque, like a picture in Dickens's "Old Curiosity Shop." '

Lady Augusta complained to the Queen of 'that stupid lameness for which warm sea baths are recommended.' Six days later she wrote:

'Sir William has prescribed warm sea baths for my stupid lameness and he advises the South rather than the North this year, we almost fear that we must give up Scotland. . . .

'It is very kind of Your Majesty to tell us of Your Majesty's reading – it makes us so happy to follow thus Your Majesty's train of thought, and dear Princess Beatrice, who is so doubly dear to us for the comfort and joy Her Royal Highness is to Your Majesty. –'

Before going abroad, Lady Augusta wrote to the Queen from Highclere Castle, Newbury:

'I had the honor to receive Your Majesty's most kind

letter before leaving home today and hasten to express
my gratitude, and to say how very keenly we rejoice in the
better accounts of Prince Leopold, the tidings of real
progress, such as so greatly to relieve Your Majesty's
mind. – We came to this lovely place today to remain till
Tuesday. I wonder if Your Majesty ever saw it or the
beloved Duchess, who had so warm a regard for the Dow.
Lady Carnarvon? – Poor Mr. Froude came with us – he
is terribly cast down by the loss of his excellent Wife and
the prospect of his long colonial voyages seems to afford
him more relief than anything else.'

And then:

'We expect to leave tomorrow (tho' it always seems
impossible the day before) sleeping at Boulogne.'

CHAPTER XIV

Lady Augusta and the Dean in France: continued
and increasing illness. Letters to the Queen. The
Dean and the Greville Memoirs. Charles Kingsley's
death. The Prince and Princess of Wales visit Lady
Augusta. The Queen's concern over her illness.
The Dean's unhappiness. Lady Augusta's death –
The sorrow of the Queen and of the Dean.

1874–5–6.

Lady Augusta and the Dean abandoned their usual
holiday in Scotland and went to the French Coast,
travelling and staying between Dieppe and Rochelle.
She wrote to the Queen from Trouville, on September
the 16th:

'We had a lovely crossing to Dieppe where we spent
some days greatly enjoying the neighbourhood of Ld.
and Lady Salisbury and their family; who have a charming eagle's nest on the cliffs close to Dieppe. We revisited
Rouen and San Fécamp which is a pleasant sea place with
a well sounding historical name – then "Etretat" which
is charming – a small Bay with very picturesque rocks
closing in at either side, and a "Plage" where from
morning to night the community bathes and swims – the
Ladies sit and work – the Gentlemen stroll about, crowds
of children play – and all talk incessantly – Such a merry
cheery world it is impossible to conceive. – The Dean had
one of his very bad headaches and was so poorly in the
night that I sent for the Dr. by means of the only living
being I could discover in the sleeping household. (There
are no bells in the Hotels!!!) Presently there appeared
thro' the darkness, escorted by my Mercury carrying a
very feeble candle – an ancient Gentleman with his face

tied up and I almost think a night cap – who had kindly got out of bed to come, and whose advice was quite what one might have expected from his general appearance! this made me the less fret when I found that my Messenger stoutly refused to go out again, and intimated that Apothecaries at Etretat could not be disturbed at night!

'. . . I am quite well except my knee – but the Surgeons say it is only tedious and I must have patience – Many people have great pain with such troubles – I must be thankful not to have that. A nephew of our friend's at Havre had derived great benefit from a rubbing Dr. at Amsterdam – but I hope the sea baths will save me from going there!'

To the Queen.

Arcachon, par Bordeaux.
Oct. 2/74.

Madam,

It was a great honor and pleasure to receive Your Majesty's gracious letter here, on our arrival yesterday.

. . . I can not describe to Your Majesty what a delight it has been to me to read what Your Majesty says of the dear young Duchess, [of Edinburgh] what a happiness to know what she was in Your Majesty's circle and how Her sweet disposition, kind, generous, open nature, and serious well-regulated mind unfolded to Your Majesty during those weeks. – It gladdens my heart to realize the satisfaction it must, I know, have been to Your Majesty to find it so, and to think what a treasure such a character is in a family. It *is* very anxious – one can but hope, and such qualities have a charm if any can have, of making up for the want of outward attractions and of winning and retaining one, of a character in many points so dissimilar.

The Dean to the Queen.

Arcachon, Oct. 4.

The Dean of Westminster presents his humble duty to Your Majesty. – He thinks that there are some points in his journey that may interest the Queen. When in Anjou he took the opportunity of going from Saumur to visit again (he had been there once before in 1851) the Abbey of Fontevrault; where, as Your Majesty doubtless remembers, are the tombs of Henry II and his Queen – Richard Coeur de Lion, and the Queen of John. (There had also been Joan, sister of Richard – the one who figures in the *Talisman* – but this perished in the Revolution) – These are the tombs which the Emperor some years ago offered to the Queen to be removed to England – on which occasion Your Majesty kindly mentioned the matter to the Dean, in reference to their being received in Westminster Abbey. The objection which the French antiquaries very naturally raised to their removal caused the Emperor to ask Your Majesty's permission to withdraw his generous offer – and it was agreed that they should remain, on condition that they should be more suitably cared for. The recollection of these instances made the Dean anxious to see what had been done to carry out this understanding. He has little doubt from what he saw that what had been *intended* to be done was quite the right thing – viz. to restore the magnificent old Norman Church, which had been cut up into compartments for the prisoners (for the whole place has been turned into a *maison centrale* for criminals) and then to place the monuments in the Church where they once had been. This restoration is still going on – but meanwhile the 4 statues remain in the same dark corner where the Dean saw them in 1851, and there is the same disagreeable process of being conducted to see them by the porter of the gaol – an exact likeness of *MacGuffog* in Guy Mannering. However they were safe from injury – and whereever they are, no Englishman can see the stately figures and majestic faces of the two kings without emotion. – And whenever the Church is finished, they will no doubt be well placed. – The history of the Abbey is very curious – having been governed by *Abbesses* who were almost always Princesses – and had a great deal of trouble in governing their monks and nuns, and also gave a great deal of trouble themselves.

From Cherbourg also was made a beautiful expedition to *Brix*, the 'stammhaus' of the *Bruce* family. – He arrived there whilst the villagers were at vespers in the parish Church. It is on a high hill, built out of the remains of the old castle which was destroyed by S. Louis, in consequence of the rebellion of *Adam* Bruce, the head of the branch that continued in Normandy, when the first *Robert* came over with the Conqueror, and from whom many of the villagers are still called Adam. – Most probably since the death of that *Adam Bruce* there has been no member of the family on the spot till the arrival of *Augusta Stanley, née Bruce,* as she left her card with the old curé. –

The Dean has heard no details of Lord Ripon's Conversion. If the son remains Protestant, it will not, he trusts, be of any lasting importance. But it was a great surprise and vexation. –

We hope that all this sea bathing will have done good

to the poor knee. It is a sad drawback to one who has had such unlimited power of movement. –

Your Majesty will understand with what unfeigned delight he has heard of the satisfaction given to the Queen by the Duchess of Edinburgh. – May all blessings rest upon her.

Our plan is to move homewards this week – and to halt for a few days as usual with Madame Mohl at 120 Rue de Bac – Paris.

From the coast they went to Paris. Madame Mohl had lent them the beloved apartments in the Rue de Bac. For a moment, it seemed, the baths and the rest had restored Lady Augusta's health; but one day, when walking in the Champs Élysées with the Dean, 'her strength gave way suddenly. She was taken home and the terrible illness followed from which she never recovered.' Madame Mohl hurried back to Paris, from Stors, where she had been staying.

120 Rue de Bac, Paris, Oct. 25.

The Dean of Westminster presents his humble duty to Your Majesty.

He writes on behalf of Lady Augusta. . . . The Queen will, no doubt, be sorry to hear that the cause of her not being able to write herself to Your Majesty and of her continued detention here is that she has been suffering for the last 10 days from a feverish attack – 'fievre catarrhal' which has kept her entirely to her room and almost to her bed. The medical man who attends her is a cousin of Dr. de Mussey (the physician of the Orleans family) of the same name and equally distinguished. – It is very vexatious that she should have been shut up during this splendid weather which she would so greatly have enjoyed.

120 Rue de Bac, Nov. 6.

The Dean of Westminster presents his humble duty to Your Majesty and begs to express his thanks for the kind sympathy of the Queen for himself and his dear wife. She now is certainly advancing towards recovery and has sat up for 2 or 3 hours for the last 3 days. But she is still very weak and cannot bear any agitation. – Next week, it is hoped that the journey may be undertaken in a separate compartment, which Lord Lytton (who has been extremely kind throughout) has procured for us – then to sleep at Boulogne – and wait for a convenient day for the passage.

The Dean has only seen the extracts from the Greville Memoirs, which have appeared in the newspapers, and which certainly were astonishing, but appear not to have contained some of the worst parts. – What struck the Dean was that in almost all the judgments which Greville pronounced on the public personages of literary or political life, experience proved him to be wrong – Lord Russell, Lord Palmerston, Lord Macaulay and (he thinks) several others. –

The Dean is much interested in hearing of Your Majesty's second Communion in the Church of Scotland, and is deeply thankful that it was so comforting to the Queen, and that there was no annoyance to interfere with the solemnity and consolation which every such occasion ought to bring with it. He has lately been studying much the history of the Sacrament and hopes some day to write something on the subject which might be of use in these days.

266

Lady Augusta to the Queen.

120 Rue de Bac, Paris, Nov. 6.

Madam,

I venture to dictate my humble and grateful thanks for Your Majesty's kind sympathy and for the beautiful extract sent to me which I have read with heartfelt emotion and thankfulness.

I have often thought of Your Majesty's severe illness since I have been ill myself. My old maid is most attentive. 'Mm. Green' tempts my appetite with morsels which would not disgrace Your Majesty's kitchen and till now I have been watched at night by a nurse from whom I have learned alleviations I never should have dreamed of; who has been to me a continual study, with a view to the education of the nurses in our Westminster 'Home.' I consider it one of the good things of this very severe trial that I shall now better understand what is needed in those who go to nurse the sick. –

Even then Lady Augusta's letters were courageous, and she wrote to her sister:

'I had been so ruffled at being tied here, and your note quite cheered me and sent me to bed to dream of delicious little mortals [Lady Frances Baillie's children] toasting before the fire and clean white nurses. . . . Had you told me it was my fault, I think I should have cried, because I have been doing everything I could think of to make myself well and strong and I never felt better in my life – no dry lips as I often have, in travelling, no feverish feeling, nothing except the little stiffness which is only the rheumaticky remains of my knee. . . . Did you really think, my darling, that I could do anything but try

267

to keep well for you and Him? . . . I do blindly what the Doctor says.'

Lady Augusta was not a willing patient. There is a letter which she wrote to her sister, which shows her impatience with her illness, and her self-assurance that she would be cured:

'Confidential. My own,

'A. is out and I am up! Fire for the first time – so much better. . . . It is *very slow.*'

To the Queen.

120 Rue de Bac, Nov. 12, 74.

Madam,

I cannot refrain from expressing the deep gratitude we have felt at Your Majesty's kind inquiries thro' Dr. de Mussey.

I never can describe the tenderness and goodness of dear M. and Mme. Mohl. While I made no progress, she could hardly bear to come near me, but her sympathy and joy now and the almost childlike way in which she expresses this goes thro' my very heart. Her husband is no less kind. Joseph daily, before his work begins, scours the markets and the butchers' shops to get me the youngest vegetables, the most delicate game, and the best meat that the town affords. These his good wife prepares for me and the kind good cook is not offended by these 'caprices de malade.' The best Bordeaux in Paris is said to exist in the cellar of Admiral Fourichon and no other will he or his wife allow me to touch. Flowers are showered upon me as if at Midsummer and everything I can think of is bought or lent. – Your Majesty sees how kind Providence is to me, and how thankful I ought to be for all the blessings

268

that I have. I was a little disheartened a week ago at making no progress towards recovery of strength – but Joseph reminded me that 'à *nos* âges on ne se remet pas si vite que quand *nous* étions jeune!'

120 Rue de Bac, Paris, Nov. 11–74.

The Dean of Westminster presents his humble duty to Your Majesty.

The Queen asks what is the nature of the malady. It is, the Dean presumes, not typhoid, but something exactly of the nature of a Roman fever. It came on in the same way – in a moment, from a chill caught on the day after our arrival here, and having overheated herself before she got into the carriage. What she now suffers from is extreme weakness and sensitiveness to the slightest agitation. The doctor says that she cannot move for eight days. Every preparation has been secured on railroad and steamer whenever the wished for day arrives.

They returned to England. The Dean's anxieties were increased by the death of Canon Kingsley, who had been perhaps his greatest friend among the Canons. Their mutual interest in letters and kindred opinions had strengthened the Dean's hand at Westminster. He died on January the 23rd, and on that day the Queen wrote in Her Journal:

'He was full of genius and energy, noble and warm-hearted, devoted, loyal and chivalrous, much attached to me and mine, full of enthusiasm, and most kind and good to the poor.'

With Lady Augusta ill and dying and himself engaged in finishing his 'Lectures on the History of the Jewish Church,' he had to face an almost unnecessary number of opinions and currents of influence in appointing another Canon. The Queen and Mr. Disraeli maintained a lengthy correspondence. Prince Leopold was ill and the Queen wanted to please him, but also her own faith in him, by appointing Mr. Duckworth, who had been the Prince's tutor. Mr. Disraeli wanted the son of Sharon Turner, the historian, and friend of his father, to be appointed, and Dean Stanley thought Mr. Duckworth's 'general qualifications . . . not quite equal to the occasion.' He wished 'Mr. Bradley, Master of University College, Oxford, previously Master of Marlborough' to be appointed. Mr. Duckworth was made Canon, but not without unfavourable criticism.

In January of 1875, the Dean wrote of Lady Augusta:

'safe, and, I trust, recovering; but very different from that indefatigable, indomitable dispenser of all good influences who has hitherto shared all my labours.'

He wrote to Madame Mohl in June of 1875:

'Our life is sadly changed – a mere ghost of its former self. But she still keeps up her cheerfulness and her patience wonderfully.'

On the 10th of October the Prince and Princess of Wales visited Lady Augusta before leaving for India, and on the next day Dean Stanley wrote to his sister:

'On the Sunday night we had a message to say that the Prince and Princess of Wales would come to take leave of us at 3.30 p.m. the next day. They came about 4 p.m., having been detained by the members of the family coming to Marlborough House.

'They brought all the five children, wishing, the Prince said, to have them all with him as long as possible.

'They all came up, and remained about twenty minutes. Fanny [1] was in the back library, and the children, after being for a few minutes with Augusta, who was delighted to see them, went to her.

'The Prince and Princess remained with Augusta and me. A[ugusta] talked with all her usual animation. They were both extremely kind. The Princess looked inexpressibly sad. There was nothing much said of interest, chiefly talking of the voyage etc. As I took him downstairs, he spoke of the dangers – but calmly and rationally, saying that, of course, the precautions must be left to those about him. I said to him, "I gave you my parting benediction in the Abbey yesterday." "Yes," he replied, "I saw it. Thank you."

'Later on in the evening Augusta wished me to telegraph our renewed thanks and renewed good wishes to the "Castalia" at Dover. I did so, and at 11 p.m. there came back a telegram from him: "Many thanks for your kind message. God bless both of you! Just off for Calais."

'It is impossible not to be affected by these thoughtful acts and kind words. Augusta was very much gratified, and none the worse for the exertion.'

The new year came, and on the first day of 1876 he wrote to Canon Pearson: 'She is much worse.' And to Madame Mohl he wrote:

'When I was speaking to my dear Augusta, she said, in the midst of her sufferings, which were then very severe, "I have nothing left but this crushed and miserable body."

[1] *Lady Frances Baillie.*

271

I said to her, "Yes, you have something besides. There is your undying love." She looked me very steadily in the face, and answered with all her strength, "That is my identity. . . . I live on and sleep." '

In the last months of 1875, the doctors knew that Lady Augusta's life could not be prolonged more than a few months. The quiet and lovely qualities of her character were the illumination of her death-bed as they were of her life. A study of her letters and journals reveals no great action in her life, no dramas of public moment. Her qualities were in her character and in her most intimate letters; there is no cruel or distorted judgment, no prejudice that was not also kind, no blame that was not tender, no opinion or advice that was not the ideal of both Christian goodness and human capability.

Her standards were inviolate for herself and for others. But she was not narrowed or made inhumane by her sense of right and wrong. While she lay in bed, with the most noble and the poorest praying for a gentle death for her then unhappy body, she worked, in the little moments of ease, with the Dean who was at her bedside. Once, as he worked on the book on the History of the Jewish Church, his courage failed a little. He was to dedicate the book to her, but he confessed his doubts of its qualities.

'Work on: work on and go to the very bottom of things and leave work that shall be imperishable,' she said. This was the key to her place in his life. Dean Stanley's enthusiasms were spontaneous and his faults were those inseparable from a keenly alert interest. Lady Augusta provided the serious urge to 'work on and go to the very bottom of things.' She herself did 'work that shall be imperishable,' for it is impossible to read all her letters without feeling that she still exists as a standard of living, a standard of spiritual consciousness, human conduct and social behaviour.

The Queen's grief over the inevitable death was terrible. All the sympathy was not needed at the Deanery. The Queen, too, was facing a terrible loss. In an age when death was made more than naturally sad by the habit of the times, she had to live on and lose almost everybody who was dear to her. She was inclined, by those same habits of the age, to sorrow outwardly over her bereavements; but they were many and those who study the story of the Queen's loneliness, with sympathy, can realise many excuses for her retirement after the Prince Consort's death. It was a tragedy which possessed her until her own death. And one of its living associations was with Lady Augusta, who was the only person who saw her and ate with her in the first terrible weeks of her widowhood. That wise, sympathetic friendship was also to end. Her sorrow intruded itself into State affairs, even before Lady Augusta's death. Mr. Disraeli wrote to the Queen, on the 11th of January, how 'distressed' he was 'to learn the sorrow which is impending over Your Majesty . . . it is the fate of Sovereigns, that the area of their affections should necessarily be limited.' He offered his sympathy 'with duty and respectful affection.'

On the 26th of February, when the Dean and Lady Augusta's relatives were too distressed at the approach of death to write any record of the end, the Queen wrote: 'Walked in the garden . . . and then drove to the Deanery.' She went 'into poor dear Augusta's bedroom, and I saw her sleeping heavily, but peacefully, not looking

273   s

much altered. I then sat a little while with the Dean, who was much upset at first. He said he only lived from day today.'

The Queen went to Windsor then, and the Dean and the little group of relations at Westminster were left to the anxious, sad days until March the 1st, when Lady Augusta died.

'My dearest friend Augusta,' wrote the Queen. 'Oh! what it means to me to lose that dear friend who was everything to me from '61 to the end of '63, being with me at those two dreadful times in '61! She was such a help in so many ways, so sympathising, loving and kind, so attached to me and mine, so clever and agreeable, known to so many. She used to write such interesting letters and knew so many interesting people. It was always a treat to me when she came. How kind she was in going to Baden – Baden the moment I telegraphed how ill dearest Feodore was, and how she did all for me there, and again at the marriage of Affie and Marie, with such zeal, love and affection!'

The Queen and the three Princesses were in the 'Abbot's pew' for the service in Westminster Abbey, where Lady Augusta was buried in Henry VII's Chapel. Her pall-bearers were the Duke of Westminster, Lord Shaftesbury for philanthropy, the Member for Dunfermline, her Scottish home, Caird for the Scottish Church, Stoughton for the Nonconformists, Motley for the Americans, and Browning for literature.

The Queen erected a memorial to her at Frogmore, beside the pretty little lake in which the Duchess of Kent's Mausoleum is reflected: a place of quiet now, of cedars and old oaks and still water, remote from everything that seems to live or breathe.

The Dean's life was emptied of all human inspiration by the death of his wife. When he went to Osborne in April of 1877, the Queen asked him to plant a tree in memory of Lady Augusta, in 'a pretty spot, near the Swiss cottage . . . a bird's nest was in a bush close to it.' He planted a Chinese juniper.

When he returned to the loneliness of Westminster, he wrote to the Queen to tell her that he had discovered that, in China and Japan, the juniper is 'regarded as the emblem of everlasting life.'

INDEX

Ada, Princess (d. of Princess Hohenlohe), 139, 157

Aix la Chapelle, 155

Aksakoff, Madame, 234

Albani, Madame, 217

Albert, Prince Consort, 25

Albert Edward (Prince of Wales), extract from letter of, 27; dinner-party at Marlborough House, lunches with the Stanleys 30; a Freemason, 105; rumours concerning, 112; his illness, 147, 166; on Sunday observance, 190; to Russia 190; farewell to Augusta, 270

Alcock, Sir Rutherford, 39

Alexander II, of Russia, 204, 205, 213, 218; visits London, 247

Alexander, Prince, of Hesse, 217

Alexandra (Princess of Wales), 30, 77; visits Denmark, 103; nurses Prince of Wales, 147–151, 193, 194, 207, 218; farewell to Lady Augusta, 270

Alexis, Prince, of Russia, 209, 217

Alfred, Prince (Duke of Edinburgh), 32; his escape, 76; grief at brother's illness, 147; suggests pale ale, 150; religious differences from those of his bride, 176; marries Princess Marie of Russia, 187–222; arrival with his bride in England, 244

Alice, Princess, of Hesse, 138, 166

Andrassy, Count, 238

Argyll, Duke and Duchess of, comment on Gladstone's attitude to Queen Victoria, 151

Arnold, Matthew, 66, 77

Arthur, Prince (Duke of Connaught), 26; in Berne, 33; goes to Russia, 190, 217

Arthur, Mr., 91

Aumale, Duc d', 174; and Bazaine trial, 183

Avignon, 58

277

ments on Bishop Temple, 116; to Germany and arrival in Potsdam, 130; received by Crown Princess, 130; comments on the children, 132; visits Berlin, 133, 134; her appreciation of Wagner, 136; at meeting of Old Catholics, 137; 'adventure' with a mouse, 141; journeys to Leeds and Peterborough, 153; letter to Madame Mohl on the death of Lady Charlotte Locker, 154; to Germany, 155; visit to Aix la Chapelle, 155; letter to Queen Victoria upon the death of Princess Hohenlohe, 156; on hospital management, 166; on *Middlemarch*, 167; on the letter of Queen Victoria to Tennyson, 169; on Lord John Russell's book, 169; her efforts to interest the Queen in persons, 170; letter to the Queen on Madame de Bunsen, 171; on the 'black singers' in Westminster Abbey, 173; helps old lady, 180, 246; letters from Berlin in

1873, 188 ff.; on character of the Empress of Germany, 196; travels extended to Russia, 191 ff.; presented to the Empress of Russia, and to Princess Marie, 203, 204; visit to the Kremlin, 232; return from Russia, and her stay in Berlin, 243; suffers from over-fatigue, 243; edits the *Journals* of the Duchess of Kent, 253, 255; calls on Carlyle, 257; returns to Paris, and is taken ill, 265; returns to England, 269; her death, 274

Stanley, Dean Arthur Penrhyn, becomes Dean of Westminster, 25; letter describing the Queen's visit, 27; disapproves of inferior literature, 30; his characteristics, 36, 49; no ear for music, 37; on marriage, 47; described by Jowett, 49; defends Bishop Colenso, 49, 74; not a mathematician, 50; his handwriting, 50; to France and Italy, 53; audience with the Pope, 61; to France, 70, 115; meeting with Thiers, 71;

INDEX